"Sitting down with *Run Strong, Stay Hungry* is like going for a Sunday long run with multiple generations of running's wisest and most-experienced. Jonathan Beverly puts you smack in the middle of a wide-ranging discussion on the sport that conveys the passion, mindset, and training methods of lifelong runners. The only disappointment is that the conversation, like a great run, must eventually come to an end."

—PETE MAGILL, running coach with 19 USA Track & Field National Masters Championships, multiple American and world age-group record holder, and five-time USA Masters Cross Country Runner of the Year

"In *Run Strong, Stay Hungry*, Jonathan Beverly interviews dozens of runners who have trained and raced hard through the decades. Their advice is clear, proven, and useful—exactly what all runners are looking for."

—AMBY BURFOOT, 1968 Boston Marathon winner,
Runner's World editor at large

"Jonathan Beverly has expertise, knowledge, and love of the sport of distance running. His book, *Run Strong, Stay Hungry,* is for runners who get that running is not about one race or rival. Running is about you, your path, and your lifetime of running."

—BILL RODGERS, four-time Boston Marathon
champion and Olympian

"Running is so challenging it makes you wise. Running is such fun it keeps you young. Jonathan Beverly captures the wisdom and the fun in his masterly distillation of the thoughts of 50 lifelong runners—that's two thousand years' experience in one fascinating book."

—ROGER ROBINSON, PhD, author and masters runner

"Jonathan Beverly mines new material in *Run Strong, Stay Hungry*. He focuses on the heroes of yesterday to learn their secrets—what contributed to their success and, perhaps equally interesting, how they failed and what they learned. A masterful read."

–HAL HIGDON, contributing editor, *Runner's World*

"If you need help getting your aging body out the door, buy *Run Strong, Stay Hungry*."

–BENJI DURDEN, coach and Olympic marathoner

"Jonathan Beverly's book, *Run Strong, Stay Hungry*, is fantastic for runners who want to continue running—and for runners who have been running for decades. I found myself nodding and saying 'Yes!' at each chapter."

–DAVE DUNHAM, mountain running champion with over 135,000 lifetime miles

RUN STRONG STAY HUNGRY

RUN STRONG STAY HUNGRY

9 KEYS TO STAYING IN THE RACE

JONATHAN BEVERLY

Boulder, Colorado

▼**velopress**®

3002 Sterling Circle, Suite 100
Boulder, CO 80301–2338 USA

VeloPress is the leading publisher of books on endurance sports. Focused on cycling, triathlon, running, swimming, and nutrition/diet, VeloPress books help athletes achieve their goals of going faster and farther. Preview books and contact us at velopress.com.

Distributed in the United States and Canada by Ingram Publisher Services

Library of Congress Cataloging-in-Publication Data

Names: Beverly, Jonathan, author.
Title: Run strong, stay hungry: 9 keys to staying in the race / Jonathan
   Beverly.
Description: Boulder, Colorado: VeloPress, [2017] | Includes bibliographical
   references. |
Identifiers: LCCN 2017027174 (print) | LCCN 2017040126 (ebook) | ISBN
   9781937716882 (ebook) | ISBN 9781937715694 (pbk.)
Subjects: LCSH: Running—Handbooks, manuals, etc. | Running—Training. |
   Runners (Sports)—Handbooks, manuals, etc.
Classification: LCC GV1061 (ebook) | LCC GV1061 .B449 2017 (print) | DDC
   796.42—dc23
LC record available at https://lccn.loc.gov/2017027174

This paper meets the requirements of ANSI/NISO Z39.48-1992
(Permanence of Paper).

Art direction: Vicki Hopewell
Cover design: Kevin Roberson
Cover photograph: Darron Cummings/AP Images; p. 261: T.L. Beverly
Interior design: Erin Farrell

17 18 19 / 10 9 8 7 6 5 4 3 2 1

To Tracy, who has taught me all I know about lifetime love, and to Landis, may you always stay hungry

CONTENTS

INTRODUCTION

The beauty of the morning and the radiance of noon are good,
but it would be a very silly person who drew the curtains and turned
on the light in order to shut out the tranquility of the evening.

–W. SOMERSET MAUGHAM, *THE SUMMING UP*

When you're 16, you don't think about whether you will still be running when you're 60. Let's face it, you can't even imagine being 60. If you think about it at all, you assume that were you to live that long, you'd have long since retired to the rocking chair.

A few quick trips around the sun and 60 doesn't feel so far away. In fact, you wonder how the years went by so fast. Many will have hung up their running shoes somewhere along the line. They'll look back at the time when they were once a runner.

But some will still be chasing it. On most days, through summer, winter, spring, and fall, they will pull on their running shoes and head outdoors. Weekdays, they'll run for an hour or so; Saturdays will find them going longer. Tuesdays they might be at the track. All of this continues a pattern they've followed for four, five, or more decades.

They're still working to get fitter and faster, even if their fast is far slower than it was back in the day. And they still compete, taking pleasure in pitting themselves against others and against the clock—both the clock ticking off the seconds of their races and the one counting down their years.

This book is about that singular group—an inspiring collection of lifelong dedicated runners whom I call "lifetime competitors."

Part of the impetus behind writing this book is certainly personal. As I move into the decades where running increasingly becomes iffy, I marvel at those who never seem to lose the fire. And while I admire those who have come late and are burning with a fresh flame, setting lifetime bests at advanced ages, I revere those whose passion, like a bed of mature coals, sustains heat after years and years of experience, successes and failures, breakthroughs and setbacks. What is the secret to that long-burning passion? Are they genetically lucky? Or are there core habits, mindsets, or practices they employ to keep the fire burning?

To answer these questions, I talked to lifetime runners I knew, then to ones they knew, and expanded to others in ever-widening circles until I'd talked to over 50 who continue to go the distance (and a dozen who had hung it up). Some of these runners were elites who had set world records and won Olympic medals. Others were more mortal and relatable, those who, through persistence and passion, arrived at regional and local racing success. I asked for their stories and listened for patterns and similarities. My goal was to find principles that superseded the particulars of their lives and could provide guidance to help others navigate the years.

What I found surprised me. It turned out that psychological perspectives are as important, or perhaps even more important, than training specifics. As nine key principles emerged, I found that these perspectives were not only important to keep running but were also key to navigating life itself: knowing yourself, making peace with your gifts, balancing priorities, avoiding the pitfalls of perfectionism, adapting to change, staying both optimistic and realistic, and accepting declining abilities without giving in or giving up. What had started as a book about running ended up being a book about life.

I consulted experts on aging, motivation, and adaptability in order to add context and theory to the personal on-the-ground stories I heard. That said, the material presented here should not be construed as scientific. It is biased by the small sample of people I interviewed and then filtered through my eyes and sensibilities. These are the eyes of a moderately competitive runner who has been running since 1977 and writing about runners for more than 20 years. For a better understanding of that perspective, read on—or else skip forward to find the principles and hear from the many exceptional men and women who are the heart of this book.

A RUNNING LIFE

Although my running fire never burned bright enough to attract much attention outside of my own, it has been steady and strong for four decades. Talking to others for the purposes of this book sent me back many times to my own story. With the 20/20 vision of hindsight, I can now see where and how I managed to avoid roadblocks and find a path that has allowed me to continue to enjoy running and compete into my 50s.

I'd like to say I was recruited for my exceptional running talent and urged to join the high school cross-country team, but in truth, running was a last refuge. After a sickly youth during which I was always overshadowed athletically by my brother, who is two years my senior, I arrived at high school. Too small for football, too uncoordinated for basketball or baseball, and a year younger than my peers, having skipped a school year in grade school, I was awkward and nerdy. So naturally, I went out for cross-country.

Cross-country is the Statue of Liberty of sport, proclaiming to the world of high school athletes, "Give me your skinny, your weak, your huddled outcasts yearning to be cool." The sport gives these misfit toys an island where they find that by applying dogged persistence, they can improve and eventually contribute—even succeed.

It was 1977 in a small coastal Maine town. The first running boom was in full flower. Fellow New Englander Bill Rodgers ruled the road-running world and was in the middle of his streak of Boston and New York Marathon victories. Joan Benoit, from just down the road in Cape Elizabeth, would set an American record in Boston in 1979.

My high school coach, Anne Norton, was a passionate convert to the running boom. She imparted a love for the act of running itself, as much or more than for racing and victories. She didn't overtrain us, set unrealistic expectations, or apply pressure for us to perform beyond our abilities. Instead, she encouraged and nurtured every runner to improve, and she celebrated personal growth at every level. Coach Norton deserves as much credit as anyone for the fact that running has remained a big part of my life ever since.

My success in cross-country and track was moderate at best. I never set a record, rarely placed in the medals, and made state only as one of the last varsity runners on the cross-country team my sophomore through senior years. But I was a contributing part of those teams, accepted and valued, something I never had been before, athletically speaking. And I loved the actual running, which served as an escape, a way to cope with adolescent emotions and crises as well as a way to become an athlete. During the stage where forging an identity is the key task, being a runner became an important part of mine.

A YOUNG MARATHONER

During the summer of my sophomore year, I ran nearly every day, and Mrs. Norton started taking me to road races. A few weeks before cross season, I ran a hilly 16-miler where I cruised comfortably past fading runners in the final stages. Mrs. Norton was impressed with my seven-minute-per-mile average. Her enthusiasm, and the congratulations of other runners, showed me that this ability to keep going was not universal, even if it wasn't as widely valued as speed.

I enjoyed going long so much that I skipped track the spring of my junior year to train for and run my first marathon—the inaugural Nike Maine Coast Marathon. I ran a 3:23, won the 18 and under age group, and added "marathoner" to my runner identity. The following summer, after graduation, I lowered that to 3:03 at the Paul Bunyan Marathon. With the arrogance of youth, I assumed 20-minute drops would be normal, that I'd run a Boston qualifier next (then 2:50), and that soon I'd be sniffing at an Olympic Trials time. None of that was true, but the marathon nevertheless had seduced me with its compelling and consuming physical and intellectual challenges.

These dreams, unrealistic as perhaps they were, led to a smooth passage over the first major hurdle runners face in keeping going for a lifetime: transitioning out of the school context of team and coach and into running on your own. I wasn't fast enough to be considered for scholarships by colleges, so I walked on to the team at a small school in Arkansas. The coach welcomed me, but within a week I determined that the commitment was more than I could handle and still maintain the grades I needed to keep my scholarships while working to cover the rest of the bills.

I quit the team but kept running, training for a spring marathon back in Maine. Running continued to be a solace, this time from the emotional hotbed of dorm life. It also provided continuity, smoothing the wildly changing patterns of my life as I tried new roles, relationships, activities, and beliefs. (Spoiler: Running would continue to provide this service during even bigger crises in years to come.)

With my focus on a Boston qualifier, I ran the first 18 miles of the Maine Coast Marathon that spring at a 2:50 pace but dropped out, fatigued from a fever I'd had a few days before. Not deterred, I immediately signed up for the Paul Bunyan two months later, but distracted by a girl, I trained inadequately, hit the wall hard, and struggled home at well over three hours.

Only 18, I decided the marathon wasn't my event and took a sabbatical from running for a few years. I ran a little and raced a little, but my focus was on college, grad school, and launching a career.

My first full-time job, directing youth programs in the Panama Canal Zone, gave me a context to run a bit more, with the kids, and to keep myself fit and sane enough to deal with them. Throughout this time, although my competitiveness waxed and waned, I still held on to the identity that I was a runner and a marathoner.

NEEDING A GOAL

That job ended abruptly a few years later, and I returned to the United States disillusioned and adrift. But what was bad for me professionally and emotionally was good for my running. The first thing I wanted to do was to train for and run a marathon. I craved an area of life I could control and a goal that could be defined and measured, difficult but achievable. The marathon was the perfect solution: simple in its lack of ambiguity and grand in its scope and challenge.

I plunged into training so thoroughly that within a few months I had broken my foot, pushing straight through a stress fracture to a full-blown crack that occurred in the middle of a 5-mile lead-up race. However, this didn't slow me any longer than the six weeks I needed to recover. I took a twisted pride in the injury and saw it as a fault of my shoes, not a personal and pervasive weakness. Within six more months, I was running a marathon, this time finishing in 3:00:34.

Throughout the next few years, during which my wife and I completed more schooling and lived in five cities and one foreign country,

I continued to run and race with mixed success. After a victory in an 11-mile trail race outside of Denver, my wife remarked, "The world has yet to see what you could do if you really focused on it."

TOP OF MY GAME

A move to New York City gave me the opportunity to test that. I fell in with Coach Bob Glover's running classes at the New York Road Runners club, and for the first time in my life, I started running at a speed and volume my high school self never could have dreamed of. Within nine months, I had smashed my PRs up to the half-marathon, stunning myself with a 1:17 at the Philadelphia Distance Run. Within a year, I was coaching with Bob, often leading the Advanced Competitive group's Tuesday-night workouts.

I was still in my 30s, so perhaps it isn't amazing that I was running so well. But many runners miss these key running years, distracted by life-building. As far as running was concerned, I was fortunate that my career was in an eddy. I worked a low-stress administrative job at NYU to pay for a PhD while dabbling in writing, and running was what I thought about from the time I woke each morning and headed to Central Park to when I put my tired, cramping legs to bed.

Even as my career took off as director of international programs at NYU's Stern School of Business and my articles were appearing regularly in running magazines across the country, I continued focusing on my training, finally cracking 3:00 for the marathon, and eventually posting a 2:46.

In 1998, another international move ensured that running would continue to dominate my thoughts. When my wife had a chance to relocate to Belgium for work, I quit my day job, moved with her, and focused on my writing. While she traveled the globe, I wrote, ran, and raced. I was in my mid-30s, setting PRs, and in the best shape of my life.

I was training to run a 2:40 in London in April 2000 when fate stepped in with another move and another opportunity. I was hired as editor of *Running Times* magazine back in the United States.

MAKING MY PASSION MY JOB

You would think being editor of a national running magazine would ensure that you are active and committed to running, but one of the dirty secrets of our sport is that the closer you get to the center professionally, the harder it is to maintain your own running. This started on the first weekend. Instead of running the London Marathon as I had planned to do, the publisher got me a bib for Boston, which was one day later.

I was looking forward to running Boston, but as you might expect, the editor of a running magazine doesn't have the luxury of sitting around with his feet up in the days before a major marathon. After working at the expo all day and attending corporate parties every evening, I arrived at the start line with tired, sore legs and shuffled to the finish in 2:55, 15 minutes slower than I'd hoped. I didn't know it then, but that would be the last time I would finish in under three hours.

In the ensuing months, I was commuting an hour to work each way and working longer and harder than I ever had. Runs became short mind-clearing bouts snuck in on early mornings. My son was born a year later, which put a stop to most of those runs, too. The few times I did race, it was painful and embarrassing, my ability far below where my mind thought my body was. I limped through two half-marathons, finishing as trashed and slow as if I had run a full marathon without adequate preparation.

DRIFTING ALONG

Had my lifestyle continued in that pattern, I would certainly have gained weight, lost fitness, and perhaps stopped running altogether. But another move, this one to the country, saved my running. In the fall of 2001, we picked up stakes in Manhattan and headed to western Nebraska. Without the commute, and having reduced my salary and role, I spent many happy miles pushing my son around the dirt roads of the High Plains.

The first year in the country, at age 38, with my son young enough to enjoy long runs with me in the stroller, I focused on the New York City Marathon, still thinking I would be able to PR or come close with a "respectable" time. A few weeks before New York, I ran Chicago as a tune-up, finishing in a comfortable 3:26. That would be my only marathon time that year, as I developed severe blisters in the first mile of NYC and dropped out, unable mentally to deal with surviving the distance.

Training became even more haphazard as my son grew. But between my day job at *Running Times* and volunteering at the high school, where I trained with the cross-country and track kids, I remained in constant contact with the sport. I was still running, and even racing pretty well in local races. I noted that I was slower but attributed it to lack of volume and focus, not my years.

NO ALLOWANCE FOR BEING A MASTER

The year I turned 40, unfazed by my age, I set an ambitious goal. In a letter I wrote to Elaine Doll-Dunn, the wife of the race director of the Deadwood Mickelson Trail Marathon, I said: "Turning 40 has given me the motivation (and my son turning 3 has given me the time) to train near the level I did in the mid-1990s, when I ran sub-2:50s. Seeing the course record at 2:52 inspired me to set that as my ideal goal, although I will be thrilled to run under 3 hours again—something I haven't done since Boston 2000, the week before I took over as editor of *Running Times*."

Training for Deadwood, I started putting in steady miles. I had hoped to build to 70-plus per week during the winter, but I found that I couldn't do that and keep up with work, coaching, teaching a community college running class, and maintaining the level of involvement with my family that I wished. So I made peace with 40 to 60 miles a week. I ran the Houston Marathon during my buildup to Deadwood, and I was pleasantly surprised to finish in 3:08 with an easy effort.

A few days after turning 40, I placed third among the masters in the competitive River Run 10K in Wichita, Kansas. My time, though two minutes off my all-time best, felt respectable, a time most 20-year-olds wouldn't be ashamed of running. And, I told myself, I was still 19th overall among 1,500 runners. Like many others, I was still drawing my esteem from how I compared to others and to my younger, fastest self.

As I immersed in Deadwood training, I enjoyed obsessing over details, calculating paces and equivalents from tune-up races, and worrying over pace adjustments for the slope of the course, what shoes to wear, what to eat the morning of the race, practicing fast downhill running on fatigued legs, checking weather reports.

I concluded my letter to Doll-Dunn: "I'm really looking forward to the run in June. Yes, it will be a race—a test of fitness and endurance. But more, it will be a celebration of six months, make that two years, of discipline, growing strength, strong, joyful runs, and youthful strength, even at 40."

The training turned out better than the race. Freakishly hot weather, peaking at over 90 degrees—the highest temps recorded for June in the Black Hills since 1952 according to race director Jerry Dunn—caused me to limp home, cramping, in 3:16. Still, I placed fifth overall.

That "still"—placing relatively well in races despite slowing times—kept me going for a long time. And what I wrote to Doll-Dunn remained true even with the disappointing results; I enjoyed the process of getting fit and using that fitness on challenging runs. I would come to learn that racing is worthwhile, if only to spur me into this process of growth.

But first, I would almost give it up.

ABOUT TO LET GO

I ran another marathon close on the heels of Deadwood and finished in 3:40, a personal worst. After that, I decided I was finished with my obsession with marathons.

I didn't quit all racing, though, and I ran a few half-marathons and 10Ks in the next year, with enough success to earn a masters trophy at the Lincoln Half-Marathon. My time there, however, was seven minutes slower than my best, and given the effort it took to run it, this came as a shock and a disappointment.

When my hip went out of whack on a run the next spring, I didn't go to the doctor—I just stopped running. When it didn't get better, I figured I was done as a runner. Two months later, my wife convinced me that I needed to run again for mental health if nothing else. So I finally sought out a physical therapist, who fixed the hip with a quick adjustment. I was back to normal, if out of shape.

I was ready to walk away from competition at this point, when age made PRs improbable and race times felt embarrassing. Injury seemed always close at hand, with old pains often present. Still looking at the world through youthful eyes, I thought masters who took their racing seriously were in denial, refusing to accept that they couldn't compete anymore, that time had moved on and they should too.

I was still deeply connected to running, however. I was editor of *Running Times*, coaching high school, and still running regularly for sanity and health. And I was fit enough that when I jumped into a half-marathon on a winter trip to Orlando, I placed fourth overall. Yes, my time was two minutes slower than it had been two years earlier, and I didn't even want to compare it with my PR, but I had felt fast, competitive, and as smooth over the distance as I remembered from my prime.

STILL CHASING IT

In 2007, I ran in the USATF Masters Cross Country Championships and the track 10,000 m. In a *Running Times* article that came out the next year about masters competition, I wrote:

> *While I claim that daily runs for fitness and mental sanity are really the reason I run, I simply don't run as much when I don't have a race to prepare for, and looming competition gets me out of bed and onto the track on a 90-degree summer morning. I like myself better when I get to the track. What is more, the older I get, the less I worry about performing poorly, and the more I enjoy the actual experience of competing, measuring myself against others, having a reason to push—win or lose, good day or bad day.*

At age 43, I was starting to let go of the absolute numbers and measure success by effort. Of course, absolute results were still satisfying, like when I'd place in the top 5 every year in a small, local 5K, my 40-something and now 50-something age nestled among teenagers and 20-somethings on the results board.

My running had certainly changed since its peak in the '90s. But so too had my attitude. After training hard for a marathon in 2009, the results were far below my expectations. Thinking I could run close to 3:00, I was again stymied by heat—what was I thinking running in Florida?—and a harder course than expected. My time was an embarrassing 3:43. That said, I still placed third overall and first in my age group. *Not bad for a man my age* was beginning to be my mantra.

Three years later, after putting in solid training with the junior high track team, I popped a 65-minute 10-miler in Denver, good for second in my age group and 36th overall in a large field. I took inordinate pride and solace in those results. Despite saying I didn't compare anymore, clearly I still cared.

Later that spring I broke a bone in my foot. This time, however, I had no intention of slowing down or backing off. I biked aggressively while wearing my boot, and a few weeks after I got it off, again won a small 10-miler. The minimalist movement that *Running Times* was covering regularly caused me to reconsider my stride, learn more about how the body works, and take seriously the supplemental work necessary to counteract the forces of my mostly sedentary lifestyle. This approach has helped me clear up old injuries, and I find I am running smoother and more pain-free than I have for decades.

I've also discovered the comfort of age grading, which I look at after every race, even after some workouts. Those numbers say I'm as good as I've ever been, staying very close to my PRs and occasionally beating them. I don't really believe that, as I know my training is considerably less, but it is still a motivating goal to pursue. The fact that I race mostly against small-town competition no doubt also keeps me going, inflating what feels like success.

I passed another disturbing threshold in fall 2016: I can no longer keep up with the top runners on the cross-country team I coach, even in training, except on easy and long runs. I could take it as yet another reminder of how old and slow I am. But instead, my point of view is this: I'm healthy, running more miles, and still have no desire to watch from the sidelines. I've yet to find anything in life that provides the same satisfaction and joy as heading out for a run and feeling like a wild horse galloping across the prairie: powerful, smooth, tireless, and fully alive and present.

The runners I've talked to who have hung up their shoes certainly all seem rational. Their argument that it had become time to focus on something else makes sense. But I can't seem to shake the obsession. I love the running too much to want to do it less, and if I'm running this much, why not take my fitness out for a spin once in a while and see what it's got?

EMBRACING TIME

As I talked with other passionate runners in the course of writing this book, my perspective evolved. I've seen more clearly that my youthful perspective on masters competitors was 180 degrees wrong. We aren't denying our age. How can we? We are reminded, every time we race, nearly every time we run, that we're slower and that it isn't a matter of being out of shape; we're not going to get back to those fast times ever again. The black-and-white certainty of time and distance forces us to face the facts with clear-eyed honesty.

Drawing the curtain and turning on the lights to block out the fading sunset would be denial. Hanging up our flats so that we can keep believing we are the same as we were a decade ago, or that we could run as fast as we used to in a fictional reality—if we had time to train more, if we weren't injured, if conditions were better—that would be denial.

I've joined those wise souls I met during this project who reject those fantasies. We know clearly that the should'ves, could'ves, and would'ves are make-believe. The "perfect" day when we are at the top of our form and all the stars align never has come in the past, and we don't have time to wait for it anymore. Today is the one day we've got, and we'll seize it with more passion than a teenager.

As I slip further into these years where I can no longer delude myself that I'm still as fast as today's youth, where I need to curtail my training to avoid injury, and where times get slower every year, I need the wisdom of those who have gone before more than ever. And so I've approached each interview with as much personal curiosity as professional interest.

I know that the thread that weaves the years of a runner's life can break easily and sometimes unexpectedly. Even as I say I want to be doing this at 90, it is mind-boggling to think that I could be running for as many years in the future as I have in the past. That road is foggy and uncertain to me, as uncertain as the path ahead was for the 13-year-old who went out for cross-country in the fall of 1977. I've started to learn the lessons of this book. I hope they will serve me as well as they have served the amazing runners I've gotten to know by writing it.

1

WHY THEY STOP

Every success story is a tale of
constant adaption, revision, and change.

–SIR RICHARD BRANSON

An important part of understanding what compels people to continue running for life, it seemed to me, was to first examine why many runners fall away from the sport.

I didn't have to look far to do my research. The list of runners who once ran often and well but do so no more is far longer than the list of those who have kept going. And although each person has a different story of how the fates conspired to remove running from their routines and identities, I quickly noticed a common theme.

People stop running when they fail to adapt, either to changing life conditions or to the demands of age. They reach a point where the effort exceeds the outcome and no longer produces the desired or expected results.

That's the big-picture reason for why they stop. But why do the wheels begin to fall off in the first place? While I found some made a decision to stop, others slowly drifted away from running as if it were a friend they'd lost contact with.

To be a competitive runner at any level requires a daily commitment. Inertia works against you; the default is *not* to run. When you're rolling, it feels easy and normal to lace up and get out every day. Running is an important part of your life—what you schedule first, look forward to, and spend much of your time thinking about.

But as soon as this consistency stops, forces begin to conspire to make it harder to restart. Schedules fill up, you put on weight, residual injuries seem to worsen with inactivity, and you lose the fitness that made running easier. Running is not necessary or convenient in today's world. You have to choose it and find the time and effort to do it.

Although reasons for stepping away are seldom simple, I found several hurdles a lifelong runner needs to negotiate in order to continue as a runner, and several reasons that convince people it is time to hang up their racing flats.

FAILURE TO LAUNCH

Moving from the structure and team context of high school or college sports to running on your own is the number one obstacle stopping runners. Close to 500,000 students run high school cross-country each year according to the National Federation of State High School Associations. More than double that participate in track.

Many of these runners, however, drop running once their four years are up. As with most high school sports, even avid participants end up moving on after school and don't adopt it as part of their adult identity or lifestyle.

Tom Luhrs of Chase County, Nebraska, was on the cross-country team for three years in the late '70s but quit running after high school. He admits he ran mostly to get in condition for basketball. He continued to run a bit for fitness after gaining weight in college and to be in shape for golf, which has been his passion since high school. Running never became part of his identity or routine, however, and he feels no sense of loss.

Tyler Talbot, in contrast, was thoroughly committed to running. He discovered a talent for distance running in junior high and led the Chase County cross-country team in high school. During his sophomore year in 2008, the team placed second in their class at state and he was the team's top finisher, coming in 14th.

"It was all I thought about for four years," Talbot said. Despite this passion, however, he stopped racing when he got to college. He had considered going to a small school where he could have run on the cross-country and track teams. But Talbot preferred the music program at the University of Nebraska in Lincoln, and he wasn't a strong enough runner to compete on their Division 1 team.

"I assumed I would have it in me to run consistently even after high school competition," Talbot said. "I thought, *I'm going to put more of my eggs in this music basket, but I'll still run, because I always have.* I didn't think it would be difficult at all."

Now 24, Talbot said he hasn't run at all for over a year and has not competed since high school. When he first arrived at college, he found a running buddy and they trained together fairly frequently, he recalls. But then his music got more demanding, and the band he was in started playing gigs out of town. He would often tell his running partner, "I can't make it tomorrow morning because I'm not going to get back until 3:00 a.m."

Talbot, now a professional musician, doesn't blame his career. "I'd love to blame it on my job, but there is time," he said. "As much as I love it, there was time, and I should have made it happen. But I didn't."

It seems that atrophy was to blame. After missing one day, then another, it didn't seem worth it to run the next. "It just snowballed," Talbot said. "It is sort of all or nothing, and I went to nothing."

As Talbot's high school coach, I can today see clues for why it became hard for him to continue. While on the cross-country team, he would do whatever was asked of him, but he was never one to train on his own. He did run with the team in the summers but struggled with the early mornings. For him, running was integrally tied to the group and friends, with little to no experience of running outside of that. That he transferred his competitive discipline to music when his team context disappeared isn't surprising. He never adopted new goals or created new habits.

Runners like Talbot don't *choose* to quit, nor do they encounter restrictions that keep them from running. Rather, it is the lack of choice that is to blame. Talbot recognizes this. "That's all it is, a decision," he said. "But for some reason there is this block; I don't make the decision to do it."

Still, running hasn't lost its appeal for him. "When I run, it still feels good, feels right," he said. "When I do get out, I feel like, Why don't I do this every day? I love it." He seemed wistful as we talked and sounded like he is likely to return to the sport. He knows he has time. "I'm still young enough to have very minimal pushback from my body."

Lots of people stop running in the context of different schedules, challenging schoolwork, a budding career, or the obligations of a young family, only to return to it later—when life settles down or they realize they crave the sport. Often the return is spurred on as a way to regain lost fitness, and only after that do they rediscover the joy of competing as well. Some get to a point where they yearn for a challenging, unambiguous goal that they can conquer to feel good about themselves. Some realize they have uncompleted dreams.

LOSING THE HABIT

Peter Gambaccini was a high school standout in track in the late '60s. He made the Connecticut state track championships twice and set the school record in the 2 mile. "It was important to me," he recalled.

But when he arrived at Dartmouth, he lost the habit. "Dartmouth didn't recruit athletes, but the fact that you were an athlete was one of the reasons you might have gotten in there," he said. "But there was no real obligation, and it was amazing how many people gave up their sports as soon as they got there."

Gambaccini tried running, but he was quickly injured and was also intimidated by the Dartmouth cross-country course. He gained the "Freshman 25," and although he lost half of it later on, he said, "I never really got in shape again and pretty much stopped running."

The running boom was beginning outside of the school context, but Gambaccini wouldn't take part in it until he was 26. "I faded into the counterculture for six or seven years," he recalled.

DELAYED DECISION

Those who do participate on a college team delay the process of making running a part of their lives as a hobby, not a requirement. But post-college, they too have a decision to make. And although they have usually run for 8 to 10 years at that point, with running becoming a large part of their identity, many stop competing or find other outlets for their competitive drives and desire to stay fit.

Brett Gooden, another talented high school runner I coached, no longer runs competitively. Gooden made state on his own several times and set the school record in the 800 m. He successfully walked on to the University of Nebraska track team.

After college, however, Gooden backed off running. "I was burnt out," he said. "I promised myself to not go for a run for an entire month after my career had ended just to (1) see if I could do it and (2) give myself time to figure out what I wanted to devote my time and energy towards."

During that month, he fell in with friends who were avid soccer players. His running speed and endurance gave him an edge, and he enjoyed the sport. "Over time, I replaced going for a run with playing pickup soccer at the pitch with my friends," Gooden said.

That fall, Gooden moved to Taiwan and became a teacher. There, he joined a community soccer league that quickly took the place running had held for him. "I was training [for] soccer at least twice a week, along with a game or tournament every weekend," he said. A few years later, he moved to Germany to pursue a master's degree and quickly found a new football club there as well.

The social, team aspect of soccer is part of the appeal, but Gooden thinks the decision is also related to the type of runner he was. "I was a middle-distance specialist," he said. "It's not often you're going to find an 800 meter road race after college. With football, I can use my speed rather than trying to keep up with guys that are five times slower than me on a track but would kill me over 10,000 meters."

Still, Gooden doesn't rule out a return to running. "I can definitely see myself coming back to running after I lose a bit of my leg speed and get older, because I'm pretty positive I will still want to remain active."

WOMEN STILL AREN'T SUPPOSED TO SWEAT (TOO MUCH)

Lifetime competitor Ann Ringlein, who coached for many years at Nebraska Wesleyan University, said that she has found that female runners are even less likely than males to continue when they leave the scholastic halls. Women often have a feeling they need to move on, Ringlein said.

She has noted in her female runners what she calls "a guilty responsibility" to use the time spent running to do something more important. She points out that societal pressures sometimes make female runners doubt themselves. They get asked questions such as, "Where are your kids?" "You get a babysitter to go do a 20-miler?"

While many female lifetime competitors shared stories about what they had to overcome to be runners in their early years, before Title IX, I had assumed this type of experience was a thing of the past, not something faced by younger runners today. Ringlein's observations, however, point to the continued different expectations for women, which she said leads some women to decide that they're not going anywhere with running and so it isn't worth their time and effort.

THINGS FALL APART

Those who hurdle the challenges of leaving scholastic running behind to become independent runners face yet another common hurdle that leads to quitting: injury.

Bob Clement had a successful high school career in Bucksport, Maine, in the early 1980s. He wasn't a star, but he improved every year until he was number two on the cross-country team and a state-qualifying middle-distance man in spring. He continued to run through college and his 20s, enough to keep fit and jump in a race a few times per year.

In his 30s, he started to run competitively again. He began running 5 to 6 miles four or five days a week and enjoyed racing for his company team, often placing in his age group.

Returning to consistent running and racing awakened a forgotten goal—to run the Boston Marathon. At age 39, Clement began training in earnest to qualify, building up gradually until he was running 13 miles a day.

One month away from his qualifier, his knee started to hurt. His local doctor called it runner's knee and prescribed rest and anti-inflammatories. But the pain didn't ease, and soon both knees were hurting. He had to give up his goal of qualifying and pull back on his running. Two years later, even walking was painful. Finally, a doctor diagnosed a meniscus tear and Clement had surgery.

"I lost over half of my meniscus in one knee and a shave from the other," he said. "After that, my left leg has never fully healed. I can manage to trot and dream of running like I did—but never more than that."

The loss of a running career from injury is common. The stories I heard mounted up quickly. But, while not discrediting those experiences, I've also heard from lifetime competitors who suffered a serious injury and found a way to continue.

We all have a different threshold for what we are willing to do and the cost and effort we will endure in order to continue running. The choices are not easy, nor are the answers always satisfying. Walking is Clement's solution, and to date he hasn't pursued any further interventions. Though he said he still misses running, he seems at peace with the decision.

OVER THE RED LINE

Others rage against the loss. Adrienne Wald is one. Wald trained six days a week and raced competitively for over 30 years. She qualified for Boston six times during her 40s and was going strong into her 50s. Then she had a ski accident in 2012 that fractured her sacrum and compressed some vertebrae.

Two years later, still unable to run, Wald had surgery, hoping it would let her run again. Unfortunately, that has not been the case. "I was running (barely) for a bit afterwards," she said. "But the fusion was not good, and I may need more surgery to stabilize my spine." She's still unable to run but said she's not giving up and that she will be back on the roads one day.

"I assumed I would be running at 100," Wald said. "I still wake up at night dreaming I am running, and burst into tears." She swims, which she finds less satisfying, but it's at least a substitute. "What I have learned from running is serving me well as I learn to adjust to the new normal for me," she said. "All the strength and discipline and positive attitude from running are really helping me cope."

Wald said that although the ski injury was the breaking point, the weakness in her spine was "found to be due to underlying osteoporosis due to under-fueling earlier in my running due to trying to be thinner and faster."

This is a recurring note for those who have to stop because of injury: They pushed the envelope too hard, too long. They didn't listen to their body and adapt.

After restarting as an adult, Gambaccini stepped away from running again for several reasons, chronic tendon issues being one of them. He believes these issues are tied to the fact that all of his training was intense. "I didn't have easy days," he said. "I would do things like run a hard 4 miles at 11:00 in the morning, then go out at 4:30 and run another hard 3. I just really liked putting the hammer down."

Shawn Love is another runner who liked hammering, and his story feels like a cautionary tale. He fell in love with running, he said, at six or seven years old, and had competed since junior high. In high school, he ran in the morning, at noon, and after school at track practice, racking up 100-mile weeks. After graduation, he was recruited by a local college but trained with a track club that included some Olympic Trials–level athletes. That's where the troubles began.

Doing track workouts, his times started dropping. But he was pushing close to the red line, working full time, going to college, and hitting the track with athletes faster than him several times a week. He ended up with stress fractures, a ruptured Achilles, shin splints, and plantar fasciitis. "I was doing way too much, too fast," Love said. "I should have cut down on the percentages of intensity, if nothing else."

Still, Love immersed himself in the sport as an official and a coach, always trying to come back as a runner. "I'd go through an injury; I'd get over it," he recalled. "First thing I'd try to do is go out and run." As an adult, he even got his 5K times down into the 15s. But he just couldn't keep it going.

"My racing was inconsistent," he said, "too much, too fast." He was coaching and doing workouts with his kids, but he'd skip the stretching and drills needed to maintain the intensity. He also blames too many hours at a desk job in his 30s, when he ate poorly and gained weight.

Although the signs are clear in hindsight, Love's breaking point came as a surprise to him. After a day of shagging shot put at a track meet in 2005, bending, lifting, and throwing the heavy balls, his back felt tight. The next morning, it was stiffer, with pain shooting down his leg. He went out for a run anyway.

"I thought, I'm just going to run through this, because I wanted to get my run in," he recalls. But the pain worsened, and he could not finish. "I stopped in midstride, and that was my last stride. I couldn't take it." A bulging disc in his spine killed his running. He's never come back.

Today he is happy just to have been able to finish a 5K three years ago. He thinks maybe if he joined a group, it would help him get back into shape, stretch, hydrate better—but he admits it is hard to start again. His memories are too strong, and he hasn't separated his identity and emotions from the paces he used to run. "When I try to go out on my own, I try to force the pace because I can sense when I'm going incredibly slow and it is embarrassing to me," he said.

Other types of exercise don't cut it. He's tried swimming and biking, but for him, they come up short. "Nothing is the same as running. No other exercise does what running does for me. I still want to run, and I miss it a lot."

"I'M PRETTY TIRED. I THINK I'LL GO HOME NOW."

Not all who quit running have a sad story. Some sound a bit like Forrest Gump out on the desert highway. After running competitively for years, it's simply time to move on.

Gerry Ellen ran for more than 25 years. She started as a miler in high school and college, then moved on to other distances as an adult. She built her life around it, from scheduling the training for months to her competitive cohort of friends.

But one day, as she was nearing 55, she stopped.

She recalls the day in 2014 when everything changed. "I was running around a lake in Austin," she recalled. "I was doing intervals mixed in with some muscle work on various benches. I felt great." But when she returned to her apartment, something felt off in her knee. The next day, it still hurt, so she did yoga instead of running.

The yoga and meditation felt fantastic. "I started doing it every day, and the next thing I knew my running dwindled to three times per week, then maybe here and there," she said. She began teaching yoga at a local health club, and eventually it was what she did instead of running.

While the pleasure of not having aching knees anymore was part of the transition, mostly it was about moving on. "I still run when I feel like it," Ellen said. "But I don't plan a day around it, nor do I get bummed out when I don't do it."

She figures it was simply a phase in her life that is now over. "It was fun while it lasted, but yoga, walking, weight training, and a 3-mile run or two here or there seems to suit me well."

Dan Williams, age 67, ran consistently for 50 years, from high school track in the '60s to road racing—including 75 marathons with a 2:32 best—and eventually ultra trail races. But like Ellen, he reached a day when he realized he was done.

That day arrived in 2011, after his 21st completion of the Western States 100-Mile Endurance Run.

"Some people, when they've run Western States, say, 'Been there, done that.' It took me 21 times and 30 years to say that," he laughs.

He's not sure whether he should take pride in his longevity or wonder about his sanity. "Fifty years is a long time to beat up your body like that."

Williams has had two knee surgeries and said they are now "beat up bone-to-bone." But what eventually put a halt to his racing was feeling burnt out from training so hard for so long, and the burden from memories of once being fast. "I stayed in shape enough to pace my friends and daughter at races. But I was just done with racing."

LOST DRIVE

Jake Klim, who ran in high school and college, continued competing after school, setting PR after PR for a decade. But one day, amid his usual regime of training hard and running strong, he lost the drive to continue.

After completing a cross-country workout with his team, he found himself thinking, *What the hell am I doing this for?* He was hot and tired, and the coach told him that he couldn't get into a marathon he had been training toward. His first thought was *I didn't really want to do that anyway.*

That reaction surprised him and sparked a realization. "I started to think, *Why was I there killing myself on a Saturday morning, for no reason— I'm not really interested in racing anymore,*" Klim recalled. "It clicked, like a light switch. I said, 'I'm done.'"

It wasn't a passing whim. "I still run," Klim said. "But I'm done with the hard training. If it's raining outside, I'm not going to run. If it's too hot, I won't go running. If it's too cold, I won't go running."

Unlike those who continue, Klim didn't find training and competing sustaining. He described it almost as serving a sentence or a tour of duty. "It is sort of like I've done my time," he said. He lists the things he's doing with the recovered time and effort. "I could sleep in, I could eat bacon and eggs and then go for a hike in the afternoon," he said. "I wanted to fill my space with other things, my brain with other things."

Klim had a second motivation to step away, one echoed by several others I interviewed, particularly if they were as fast as he was and used to finishing at the front of races. The better you are, the harder it is to accept that you're never going to be faster. Your hardest effort, after the most dedicated, structured training you can do, will be slower and farther back in the pack than you used to be.

"I didn't want to be that guy who is clinging on," Klim said. "I know that guy or woman—hobbling around, getting injured, climbing back to run these times that are inferior to what they used to run."

By his mid-30s, Klim felt he had reached the top of his game and that all paths now led downhill. "It was hard because I wasn't what I used to be, and there was no way to get back to where I used to be. It would require a herculean effort that would result in another injury, if it was even doable at all."

Klim walked away while he was still faster than most ever dream to be—running 10-milers in 52 minutes—but having achieved a certain level, for him, anything less was failure. He recognizes that others make different choices, and he gives them kudos for continuing to grind it out. "Maybe they're the winners and I'm the loser for not holding on," Klim mused.

ALL OR NOTHING

Mark Mastalir was the best high school miler in the United States in 1986, clocking a 4:05.6 mile as a senior. Six years later, in 1992, he stepped away, never to compete again.

Mastalir had a difficult transition to college, where the coach took a very different approach than what had worked for him before. It took him four years to run faster than he had as a senior in high school. During his last year of college eligibility, he ran a 3:41.30 1500 m and qualified for the 1992 Olympic Trials in New Orleans. At the trials, however, he failed to make the final.

"I ran as hard as I could and didn't make the team, and that was kind of the end," he said. "I had reached the pinnacle of what I thought I could do, so it was time to move on and do other things."

Mastalir stayed close to the sport, working for Reebok, which had sponsored him as an athlete, and still running. Working in Boston, he'd often go for 10 to 15 miles along the Charles River. "I was in great shape back then. I didn't compete, I didn't have the desire, but I still ran pretty much every day."

But without the goal of competition to compel his training, he started to let it slip away. "It just diminished," Mastalir said. "I lost the desire to compete, then I lost the desire to train."

Today, at age 49, he's had a couple of knee surgeries and hopes to get back to simply being able to run some for fitness.

Grant Robison stayed with it longer than Mastalir, but his end point came at the same place: the Olympic Trials. Robison, who was a star runner since grade school, ran the third-fastest all-time mark in the 1500 m at Stanford and competed in the 2004 Athens Olympics 1500 m.

Following a breakup with his wife in 2007, he poured his emotional energy completely into training for the Olympic Trials to be held in Eugene in 2008. "It was a little bit of an outlet for that, something else to focus on," Robison recalled. "I put all my chips in."

When he finished 12th in his semifinal heat and failed to make the final at the trials, it was over. "I was emotionally fried," he said. "I threw my spikes in the trash. I didn't cool down. I was just done. I didn't run for eight months, not even a step."

It wasn't just missing the goal of joining the Olympic team, however, that pushed him over the edge. Robison said he was nearing the end of what running had been in his life.

"It was a money issue too," Robison said. Reebok had stopped sponsoring him in 2006, so he was working at the Playmakers shoe store in

Michigan and trying to fit training around work. "I know people can do that and do it well," he said. "I don't think I have the fortitude, the dedication to get up and get the training in before or after work hours."

Heading into the trials, Puma had indicated it would sponsor him if he made the team, which would have allowed him to focus fully on running. "So it was all things combined," Robison said. "I got a divorce, didn't make the final, didn't get a contract. I was ready to be done."

In talking about his running, Robison reveals other clues for why it was all or nothing for him. "I always loved racing. That was why I went to practice," he said. "I didn't really love going for a run. That was part of the necessary work to be competitive and reach the goals in the racing arena."

Running had always been results-oriented for Robison, and in pursuing competitive excellence, he pushed himself harder than most of us ever will. Eventually, he just burned out.

A year after walking off the track in Eugene, Robison decided to give running another try. "I'd put on my shoes and walk down the street, and I'd think, *I just don't want to go for a run*, and I'd walk back and take my shoes off," he recalled. He talked himself into it a few times, but when it came to doing speed work, he didn't enjoy pushing himself anymore.

Today, he says that he has run maybe twice, total, in the past year. He doesn't want to get a belly, so he has a goal of running two to three times per week, just to break a sweat and stay healthy. But he says it's a challenge to schedule and make the time without that competitive motivation.

Still, he doesn't see himself returning to racing or chasing masters goals as he approaches 40. "I think I'd have a hard time being able to incorporate the aging process and being okay with myself in that regard," he said. "I don't know that I could be all that excited in running an 18-minute 5K, even if that could be like a great achievement for me. I don't see that as being a big incentive for me."

Instead of returning to running, he's finding himself drawn to other sports. "I want to try my hand at tennis and see if I can be decent at it. Or try to learn a golf swing. That seems to be a draw these days: Try something new." On the track, he simply can't get away from the ghost of his past. For a runner like Robison, you are either at the top or not in the game at all.

NO GOALS LEFT

For anyone accustomed to being at the front of the pack, the slightest decline can cause you to wonder if it is worth continuing.

"I literally had no goals of any sort. I had set my PRs, and they weren't going to improve," Gambaccini said about how he felt when he was 37. While still the top runner in his club, he knew he was reaching the end of his best years. "It was all about the numbers for me, and wanting to do better." So as soon as his times started slipping, such as the day he gave his all and ran a 25:06 for 5 miles when his PR was 24:35, he started thinking about quitting. "*Well, this is as good as you're going to get,*" he recalled thinking.

Looking back, now far out of shape, Gambaccini marveled at his youthful arrogance. "Can you imagine that you're not happy running 25:06 for 5 miles? What kind of idiot was I?"

But he knows he failed to make that transition from always getting better and being at the front of the pack to being simply fit and strong for his age, the best he could be given the time and energy he could devote to the sport. Gambaccini had no goals left and failed to adapt or find new ones.

Elite runner Joe LeMay, who placed second in the 10,000 m 1988 US Olympic Trials and once ran a 2:13:55 marathon, came to this same point about the time he turned 40, when he found he couldn't maintain the training level he'd achieved for years.

"I continued to run, I just didn't train 100 miles per week. I'd train 30 to 40 miles per week," LeMay said. "It wasn't that I no longer wanted to; I couldn't, without getting injured. I'd strain my hamstrings or pull my calves."

LeMay, who missed the Olympic team twice due to arcane rules, was known for his gritty determination and intense, methodical training. Soon after he ran that marathon PR, on his 33rd birthday in 1999, he said in an interview in *Running Times*, "I think about retiring all the time. With all the injuries I get as I get older, it becomes less and less fun. If I can't train with the dedication I'm used to, I'm not interested in training at all."

LeMay wasn't interested in age groups, masters competitions, or age grading his times. He admitted that his definition of success in running is fixed. So he's transferred his competitive energies to rowing, where he doesn't have the weight of his younger running self hanging about his neck.

"I'm not comparing with what I used to row 20 or 25 years ago," he said. "Because I'm new to it, I have a lot more enthusiasm for the sport than I might otherwise have if I had been doing it since I was in my early 20s."

THINGS GET IN THE WAY

In chronicling the steps of his retirement, LeMay also revealed another hurdle that seems significant.

After he turned 30, he continued to run, eventually setting that marathon PR, but then he got a new job with a long commute. He didn't see how he could handle the commute, work all day, and still go running on the twice-a-day schedule he was used to. So he quit.

People often fall away because of something getting in the way. LeMay's reason is not unique—many runners fall out of the habit because of a new job with more hours, or having kids, or a change in relationships.

For Gambaccini, it was a difficult relationship. "I was with someone who was disruptive to my lifestyle." Gambaccini said. "I was lucky if I got any sleep in."

He got out of the caustic relationship eventually, but by then the damage to his running had been done, making it much harder to come back. "If you start to slip, you can slip really far," he said. "I ate poorly. I gained an enormous amount of weight. I got lethargic. Scar tissue formed on old injuries and became a problem."

After Mastalir walked away from competition, he kept running, and he might have returned to the sport had he not fallen out of the habit because of his hectic work and travel schedule.

Mastalir said, "I'd rationalize, *If I can't go out for an hour, I'm not going to run.* Then it became, *If I can't go out for 45 minutes, I'm not going to run.* Then it became 30 minutes. All of a sudden, I kind of stopped running."

When things get in the way, many runners tend to look back with nostalgia and regret.

"We're like earthbound creatures, and we don't really want to be," Gambaccini said. "I miss any sensation of floating at all."

"I want to start running again," Mastalir said. "It is the easiest thing you can do, just lace them up, head out the door, and it is simple and raw and real. I'm passionate about the sport of running. I just got on a bad path to not running so much."

There is nothing wrong with being once a runner. Moving on to a new focus, finding health and happiness elsewhere can be the right path for many. But for those who want to continue, or to return, and can't find the way past the roadblocks, the loss is sad, even devastating. Before I get there, before you get there, let's turn to those who have successfully made the transitions, avoided the pitfalls, and sustained their fire and ability through life's decades.

THE KEYS PART ONE

PHYSIOLOGICAL PRINCIPLES

2

CONSISTENCY
MAKING RUNNING A HABIT

To be a consistent winner means preparing not just one day,
one month, or even one year–but for a lifetime.

–BILL RODGERS, FOUR-TIME WINNER OF THE BOSTON
AND NEW YORK CITY MARATHONS

If you run south from the center of Lamoine, a small town on the coast of Maine, you'll find yourself on the Shore Road. A narrow strip of pavement, lacking even a painted center line, it winds among trees and quaint houses as it draws a rough circle around the western edge of the Lamoine peninsula. Occasionally you catch glimpses of the mountains of Acadia National Park in the distance, but you never reach the shore. Eventually you connect to Route 184, a slightly larger highway, and, turning left, soon arrive back at the Grange, 4.25 miles after you started.

The route is pretty, but mostly unremarkable. This loop, however, has a history. One summer evening in 1967, Robin Emery ran around it. She hasn't stopped since.

In '67, Emery was a 20-year-old coed at Allegheny College in Pennsylvania. The house where she now lives, next to the Lamoine Grange Hall, was her family's summer home. In those pre–Title IX days, she had no competitive sporting opportunities. Emery, a tomboy who outran the boys throughout her childhood, chafed under this discrimination.

"Young ladies weren't supposed to do that kind of thing," she told me while sitting in her kitchen, the walls papered with race photos, framed results, and awards dating from the 1970s to the present. Women were considered fragile, she said, and society didn't have a place for an athletic female. Adopting the voice of stodgy matron, Emery mocked, "You're not supposed to sweat. Boys won't like you if you beat them."

One summer night, she started walking around "the square," the 4-mile loop from the summer house, and decided she'd see if she could run it. "The next night, I did it again," she said. "And that was it, ever since. Haven't looked back."

Emery continued running when she returned to college, often at night, on a golf course, or in a cemetery, wearing bulky sweatshirts to avoid unwanted stares and catcalls. The following summer, she again ran endless loops of "the square" back in Lamoine.

Eventually, she started entering races, and as the only woman, naturally, she won. But even when other women joined the ranks, she continued to win. Indeed, the first time she got beat was in the 1976 Portland Boys Club Race—by a precocious teenager 10 years her junior named Joan Benoit.

Emery kept running and competing through her 40s. She ran many of her best times as a master. "I was flying," she said of her running during that time. The Maine Running Hall of Fame estimates that she won 255 races, one of the last being her 14th victory at the Bangor Labor Day 5-Mile Road Race, at age 51.

Eventually, the elite victories dried up, but that didn't stop her. She kept running and racing through her 50s, then 60s, channeling her competitiveness into winning her age group. Today, at 70, she's chomping at the bit to garner more age-group awards.

"I'm too dumb to stop!" she laughed.

Emery is the consummate lifetime competitor. She started in her youth and 50 years later is still competing, racing, and working passionately to be her best.

What is the key to her longevity?

DEVELOPING THE HABIT

Those endless loops of her 4-mile "square" hint at the first key to running strong for a lifetime: consistency.

From the beginning, Emery has run consistently. What started as something she *could* do quickly evolved into something she *wanted* to do every day, and eventually something she *had* to do.

"It was beginning to be a habit back then," she said, describing her early years of running. "Kind of hard not to run. I'd get really depressed."

That habit hasn't waned. Emery still runs every day, often the same loop that she first ran more than 50 years ago. She runs through Maine winters and summers, through aches and pains, and through the years that have slowly robbed her speed. Contemplating what keeps her going even now, she admits it probably has to do with what she calls an addiction to running.

"I haven't missed a day in like three years," she said. "It's like eating. It's like breathing. I can't not run."

Consistency is a universal feature of lifetime competitors' training. These are people who run often—sometimes daily, or even twice daily, every week of the year, year after year.

It perhaps sounds axiomatic to note that the key characteristic of lifetime runners is that they run. But indeed, consistency lies at the very heart of their long-term running success.

American running icon Bill Rodgers, sometimes referred to as "King of the Roads," offers another compelling portrait of consistency. Rodgers won both Boston and New York four times and set masters records throughout his 40s. Having risen to the top of the sport, Rodgers continues both to run and to care as he approaches 70, whether he's doing 140-mile weeks and running 2:09 marathons, as he did in his 20s, or getting in 6 miles a day and happy with a 1:47 half-marathon, as he is today.

"I was running twice a day from age 26 to my late 40s," Rodgers said. "At 40, I was still doing some doubles, getting in 100-mile weeks."

Rodgers estimates that he's run more than 180,000 lifetime miles, and he said that for 15 years in his prime, he never missed more than three days.

Today he runs six days per week, about 40 to 60 miles total, with no intention of stopping. When asked if there was any time when he thought that he'd done enough, he responded with an impassioned no. "I'm one of those people who needs to run. I'm a runner for life."

Rodgers had to run a lot of miles to be elite. As important as that volume, however, has been his consistency.

ADDING IT UP

Many lifetime runners have accumulated 100,000 or more miles. Reaching such a total doesn't happen in short, impassioned bursts of mileage. It requires running consistently high mileage every week, every year.

Dave Dunham, a 52-year-old from New Hampshire with elite running credentials on the roads and mountains, has kept a log since his first week of training for track in 1978. An accountant with the US Treasury, he keeps track of just about everything: daily miles, race times, injuries, even his win/loss record with his buddy Dan. So he can quantify what that kind of lifetime of running means in terms of consistency.

"I've done 133,000 miles lifetime, which is about 9.5 miles a day since December 1978," he rattled off. "Thirty-two hundred miles a year average. That's with days off."

For decades, he typically ran about 100 miles per week. Since turning 50, he's cut back his miles due to concern about his ankles. He still runs plenty, though, about 80 miles a week. "I do a lot of doubles, and then a longer run on the weekend," he said. He'd like to do even more but said he can live with 80 per week, if he disciplines himself.

Sixty-three-year-old Reno Stirrat boasts a lifetime total of more than 158,000 miles. In 2016, he ran 3,275 miles despite spraining his ankle and having to wear a boot for several weeks that fall. Stirrat has been going long since he spent a year in the US Marine Corps between high school and college in the early '70s.

In college, he upped his miles to 120 to 130 per week, settled down to 90 miles for several decades afterward, and today says he does about 80. He runs only once a day, so his runs average over 10 miles, with a weekly long run of 16 to 18 miles, whether he is training for a marathon or not.

Those consistent miles have carried Stirrat to sub-3:00 marathons in every decade since the '70s. Indeed, he's one of only a few who have run sub-2:45 in each of the last five decades, with a personal best of 2:19, and he aims to be the first to break 3:00 for six decades when 2020 rolls around.

SOMETHING EVERY DAY

Rodgers, Dunham, and Stirrat are elite runners and have built up their ability to handle lots of miles. But consistency is a trait common to all lifetime competitors, even if their totals don't always add up to those high elite levels.

Craig Christians, 56, of Omaha, has been running since 1978, his sophomore year in high school. He considers his running above average, but not in the same league with elites.

But this has never deterred him. He was hooked from the start, even running a marathon his senior year of high school. He went on to run in college, upping his miles to between 50 and 70 a week and developing a daily habit.

Christians has all his miles tallied on a spreadsheet with multiple tabs for PRs and lists of races in each decade. It reveals an average of 1,561 miles per year over the past 40 years. Many of the years fall close to that total, with only three lower than 1,000—injury years offset by a few stellar ones over 2,000.

Fifteen hundred miles per year works out to an average of 30 miles per week. No single 30-mile week sets the world on fire, but 2,080 of them have made Christians a solid, consistent competitor over a lifetime.

"If I were physically able, I can't think of ever taking more than a week off at any time," Christians said. "I am the church of consistency. I'm the leader of that church."

Christians definitely views consistency as one of his keys to longevity. "Just do something every day. It's that simple," he said. It doesn't have to be backbreaking or lengthy, he continued, adding that his mantra has become "it's never a bad idea to go for a 30-minute run."

EXTREME CONSISTENCY

Some, finding in consistency a key to success, then take it to an extreme. A passionate subgroup of runners includes those who have gotten in at least 1 mile per day, every day, for decades.

While some notable runners have held long-term streaks, such as Olympian Ron Hill, who ran every day for 52 years, streaking is actually quite uncommon among the lifetime competitors I interviewed. Kent Lang, 55, of Missouri was one of the few who maintained a significant streak. Lang said he's always tended to run every day, going three to four years at a time without breaks. His current streak of consecutive running days as of this writing dates from February 2006.

Not only is Lang consistent, but he also racks up a lot of miles for a sub-elite runner. During the '80s and '90s, while in his 20s and 30s, Lang often ran 90- to 100-mile weeks. Now 54, he still puts in 50 to 60 miles per week and says there has never been a day when he thought, *I don't want to run today.*

Lang admitted that as he's aged, he's found that minor injuries nag him, such as a recent bout of plantar fasciitis, but these haven't stopped his streak. "I haven't missed a day of running in over 10 years, so I'm not going to let a little PF make me stop," he said. "And if that means I hobble through a 2-miler because my PF hurts, then that's the way it is going to be."

In contrast, several lifetime competitors were adamantly against a daily compulsion. "I hate the streak thing," said Budd Coates. "I've never been afraid to take a day off."

Coates, 60, is not only a lifetime competitor but also a longtime coach and a trainer with Rodale and *Runner's World*. He believes in rest days, as well as crosstraining, to maintain consistency. "You don't have to run every day to enhance your fitness," he said. "You can crosstrain, you can use the spin bike, you can use the ElliptiGO [a combination of bike and elliptical trainer]."

Streaking has its pros and cons. Running every day is a great way to make running a nonnegotiable, automatic habit. It is also a viable goal and inspiration on its own, as it is for former Olympian Benji Durden, now 66, who took up streaking in his late 50s, following cancer diagnosis and treatment.

On the flip side, however, when streaking becomes the main goal, it can limit a runner's performance and competitiveness. If preserving the streak is the focus, then you may find yourself reluctant to push closer to your red line and risk having to miss a day. Streaking can also be a good way to get injured or exacerbate an injury, simply because of the nonnegotiable mandate.

REST DAYS

Several lifetime competitors, while consistent runners, also praised the benefits of taking days off.

John Mirth, 54, believes a key to his longevity stems from having learned early in his running life that he needs rest days. An engineering professor in Indiana, Mirth has a 2:19 marathon PR and has sustained a high level of fitness for four decades.

"I've had pretty good consistency," Mirth said. "Every year since I've started running, I've been able to run over 2,000 miles per year." Usually his total has been far more than that, with several years over 4,000, and many in the high 3,000s, or an average of 10 miles a day.

A few years after he got out of college, Mirth's work schedule forced him take one day off a week. While at first reluctant, he was surprised to see that it improved his running, and he credits this day off, at least in part, for his continued ability to run high mileage through the years.

Masters miler Leonard Sperandeo, 56, of Sacramento, California, was once a streaker but stopped running every day after he turned 50. "A day off is critical, the older you get," Sperandeo said, "for your mind, if not your body."

This pattern was borne out in several others I interviewed. Needing more recovery, they increased their rest days as they aged, which meant one or two days off a week.

Lifetime competitors, even those running most days or even twice a day, also take more extended time off when they need to. At the height of his career, running doubles and 140-mile weeks, Bill Rodgers says he took breaks.

"If I had a twinge in my calf or Achilles, I'd take three days off and go to the exercise bike or pool," Rodgers said. "Then I'd come back and I'd run 1 mile or 2. The next day, 2 or 4, then 6 or 8. So let the body recover, ramp up."

Looking back, Rodgers reflects that he should have taken even more breaks. "I only took that time off because I was injured," he said. "It probably wasn't adequate. We didn't rest enough," he said, referring to himself and other elites who rose to fame during the '70s running boom.

Fellow Boston Marathon champ Amby Burfoot, 71, follows a similar three-day-off strategy in response to a twinge. And, like Rodgers, he wishes he had learned to take breaks earlier in his career. Obsessed with maintaining high mileage, he'd run through mild injuries when he was younger, often making them worse, and didn't learn the three-day rule until he was a master.

The bottom line is that serious runners take days off, either scheduled or as they feel they are needed. Running consistently doesn't have to—and in many cases, shouldn't—mean running daily.

＝

WHY IT MATTERS

Runner after runner revealed that they have run often, every week, month, and year for decades. Is this simply a sign of their shared passion, or is this kind of consistency actually key to their performance and longevity?

Research confirms the significance of consistency for masters runners. In a study published in the December 2008 *Journal of Sport and Exercise Psychology*, researchers questioned participants in the US and Canadian masters track and field championships about their performances and training throughout the years. They found that the most reliable predictor of performance was the amount of training done consistently over the past five years.

"Middle-aged athletic individuals who retain a high level of performance do so likely because they have maintained years of uninterrupted practice, consistently have shorter off-season periods, exhibit higher weekly amounts of practice, and avoid injury," researchers concluded.

The study also found that while the training that masters runners had done in the few months just before their races was a better predictor of their results than either age or early-life training, it was not as important as what they had done during the five years prior. A solid block of consistent training in the years prior to the performance made the most difference.

The research revealed that successful masters athletes have learned that they must train "systematically and continually" in order to maintain their skills and fitness.

Steady Dose

It isn't just masters who benefit from being systematic and continual. Consistency is an essential key to running better at any age. In his comprehensive work *The Lore of Running*, sports scientist Tim Noakes named "Train Frequently, All Year-Round" as the first law of training. "What is really required is a little exercise constantly; this will benefit you permanently to a far greater degree than a single heavy dose at long intervals," he wrote.

Running regularly allows you to get in more volume and adapt to that volume so that it becomes normal. Anytime you fall off, you have to rebuild your capacity for work, a slow and risky process.

Steve Kartalia, a lifetime competitor still racing at the national level in his 50s, learned the consistency lesson the hard way. After steady improvement in high school, his college running was disappointing due to a continuous up-and-down cycle of injury and recovery. Post-college, with the help of his coach, he found a level of effort that allowed him to maintain more consistent training.

That new level meant pulling back a little from his collegiate training load. His coach told him to run 60 to 70 miles a week, an amount he'd shown he could maintain without injury, instead of the 80 to 90 that regularly put him on the disabled list. "It may take you longer to get fit, but once you get there, you'll be able to race and keep racing and keep improving, rather than dropping back to an earlier point in the process," his coach assured him.

> *What is really required is a little exercise constantly;*
> *this will benefit you permanently to a far greater degree*
> *than a single heavy dose at long intervals.*
> —TIM NOAKES

Sticking to the plan took patience and restraint. But Kartalia was able to build confidence and fitness through a newfound consistency, uninterrupted by the setbacks he had experienced before. Under the new strategy, he said, "I didn't get injured, and my times just kept dropping."

Four years later, Kartalia ran an Olympic Trials qualifying time in the 10,000 m. Kartalia's continued success as a master stems from learning this lesson of consistency in his youth.

Avoiding setbacks and the need to restart is especially important for the masters athlete. "Fitness is easier to retain than to gain," said coach Greg McMillan, author of *You (Only Faster)*. "As we age, regaining it becomes more and more difficult—physically and mentally. So, runners who have had a long successful running career are the ones that just keep racing. They keep training. And, they race lots of distances and do lots of different types of training. Use it or lose it seems to come to mind and these athletes continue to 'use it' so they never lose it."

Whenever you take a break, even for as little as a week, running feels harder when you return to it. Christians tells about taking a couple of weeks off after a race to rest a groin injury. "Even after two weeks," he said, "it is like, 'Damn, I've never run before.'" It takes a few days of running to get back to normal, and a few weeks to reach the same comfort with the training volume.

At some point, we've probably all experienced the feeling Christians expresses, and it isn't just in our heads. Coming back after time off *is* hard on your body. Multiple recent studies in a variety of sports have shown that it's harder to increase training volume than to maintain it. The studies suggest that what we've typically called "overuse injuries" would be better named "training load injuries." In other words, it isn't regular volume that causes the injuries, but spikes.

A 2016 study out of Australia showed that athletes who maintain a steady, high load of stress are less likely to get injured than those who have less volume of training. But if you increase your weekly load by 20 percent more than the average of the past four weeks, you slightly increase injury risk, and that risk becomes three to five times greater if you have a spike of 50 to 60 percent.

Interpreting these studies, professor of exercise science Tim Gabbett argued in the *British Journal of Sports Medicine* that chronic undertraining accompanied by overloading spikes is more likely to lead to injury than sustained heavy workload, which can actually protect against injury.

In another 2016 article in the same journal, researcher Mick Drew of the Australian Institute of Sport in Canberra wrote, "Labeling these injuries as 'overuse' may encourage athletes to reduce their training unduly, thus exposing their tissues to deconditioning or an inconsistent loading pattern which have been associated with injuries."

It's Getting Up to Speed That Hurts

Signs indicate, then, that it isn't volume that hurts us but ramping up to that volume too quickly. If a runner wants to run at the mileage necessary for high performance, the safest way is to build up gradually then stay at a relatively high volume over time. Inconsistency leads to having to build back up continually, thus increasing risk.

There's another reason inconsistent training hurts our ability to run. "When we lay off, we gain weight," said Coates. "Even if we don't gain weight, our bone density and muscle mass are affected in a negative way. When you take time off, you lose what is great and strong about your body. So now, when you start back, if your bone density isn't what it was and your body fat is higher than what it was, you're going to be less efficient. Which makes it biomechanically more difficult."

McMillan has a similar perspective on the issue. "Consistent training seems to also help with weight gain (avoiding it), mobility (maintaining it), and strength (gaining it)."

When you take time off, be it a week, a month, or a year, your return to training is harder and you're more likely to get injured as you ramp back up. The older you get, the more difficult this process becomes. After the difficulty of having to come back from foot surgery in 2013, author and lifetime competitor Scott Douglas said, "There's no way in hell I could have started running at 50."

Many I talked to who had quit running blamed the perils of inconsistency. When small breaks become longer breaks, you begin to lose fitness and gain weight. At that point, you can't pick up where you once were, everything feels harder, and it is too easy to just accept that you are over the hill and have become a former runner.

In contrast, those who maintain a constant level of fitness are often able to continue year after year, even at high mileage, because their bodies are adapted to that level of effort as "normal." As Douglas put it, "It's easier to run 50 miles a week than 20 miles a week." The consistency makes you stronger, which makes each run easier, which makes doing the next one easier in a self-perpetuating cycle.

*Those who maintain a constant level of fitness are often able to
continue year after year, even at high mileage, because their bodies
are adapted to that level of effort as "normal."*

"Runners intuitively know this," Gabbett said when I interviewed him. "If they can run consistently, train consistently, it actually builds robustness, it doesn't build fragility."

WHAT SHOULD I DO TODAY?

For lifetime competitors, running regularly is a habit. It's not something they have to force themselves to do or that they have to choose anew each day. It's a given in their lives.

In *The Power of Habit: Why We Do What We Do in Life and Business*, author Charles Duhigg explains that a habit is a mental loop that plays automatically in response to a certain cue. And once a habit is formed, it becomes the default.

"When a habit emerges, the brain stops fully participating in decision making," Duhigg wrote. "It stops working so hard, or diverts focus to other tasks. So unless you deliberately fight a habit—unless you find new routines—the pattern will unfold automatically."

When running becomes a habit, the default is to get out and run. But habits don't happen by luck—they happen when you create a pattern. Initially, we have to choose to run consistently. It helps to tie it to a cue, like seeing running clothes laid out every morning, or piggyback it to a habit you already have, such as stopping at a park you drive by on the way home from work every evening.

Before long, you begin to find that running, and the good feelings it creates, are a crucial part of your day. That good feeling is imperative to creating a habit and sustaining one. Duhigg explains the reason you continue a habit is because that habit results in a reward that you begin to crave. He reports on a 2006 study at New Mexico State that found the reason people continued to exercise was because of how it made them feel. Running made them feel good, or it gave them a sense of accomplishment.

Runners know this. Emery reflected what virtually every long-term runner said about why they continue: "It just feels so good," Emery said. "How you feel when you run, how you feel when you don't run: Compare those."

The key to making running a habit rather than a daily choice is to do it long enough and regularly enough that you miss those feelings when you don't run. The habit then delivers the reward (good feelings) and in turn leads to running with consistency and excellence.

To Make a Habit

How long does it take to form the habit? A 2009 study out of University College London found that people required an average of 66 days before an activity, repeated in a "consistent context," became automatic. But that time frame varied considerably, ranging from 18 to 254 days. Take note, however, that forming the habit didn't require streaking. Missing one day didn't derail the process. But it has to be regular enough to become the default rather than the exception in your routine.

Kelly Kruell, a 58-year-old attorney in Portland, Oregon, has been running nearly daily since high school, averaging 70 miles a week for many of those years. "Unless I have a good reason not to, I'm running every day," she said. "It has just happened forever. I don't even think about it."

Kruell's work and family schedule is too erratic for her to run at the same time every day, but that doesn't deter her from making sure she runs.

For her, it is never about *if* she will run that day, it's about when and where. "It could be 11:00 at night, could be early in the morning, could be lunchtime. I'm flexible about when it happens, but it will happen. You've got to get used to that."

HOW MUCH IS ENOUGH?

So just exactly how much running how many days a week is sufficient to qualify as *consistent*? That's hard to pinpoint. But the lowest mileage I heard from lifetime competitors, even those in their 70s, was 25 to 30 miles, running five days a week.

When they talk about this lower limit, it agrees with my own experience; you need roughly that much consistency to feel like a runner. By "feeling like a runner," I simply mean an internal feeling that you can run comfortably, at your natural pace, for long enough to be immersed in the run. In later chapters of this book, I'll talk more about the importance to lifetime competitors of achieving this "tireless state," as legendary New Zealand running coach Arthur Lydiard called it. For now, note that consistency is not only a way to improve your race times and stay healthy but also necessary to achieve the physical transformations that make running comfortable and joyful. Once you've discovered this, consistency is both a way to maintain the fitness that enables it and a way to experience that fitness regularly.

Although some may view lifetime competitors as highly disciplined and driven, for people who make the difficult choice to run consistently, day in and day out, in order to train toward their goals, quite the opposite is the case.

Said Mirth, "Sometimes people find out how much I run, and they say, 'I admire your discipline.' I tell them that I don't have any discipline. Running is on autopilot. I run because I run—I'm not disciplined enough to stop."

It may take discipline to create a habit, but once ingrained, it becomes harder to quit than to maintain it.

Choosing Running

To run consistently through the years will sometimes require choices. No matter how disciplined you are or how much you love running, if your career or commute take all of your available time and energy, you won't be able to maintain the habit. At some level, every lifetime competitor has chosen running over something else, and runners often factor the time desired for running into life decisions such as their career path or where they live.

It takes discipline to create a habit, but once ingrained,
it becomes harder to quit than to maintain it.

Daniel Grimes, 58, an Idaho resident, once happily turned down a promotion because it would have required him to work three more hours a day, which he didn't want to do, in part because it would have reduced his running time. Durden could have gotten an advanced degree and a high-powered US Navy job, but he didn't because nothing ever compared to running. "What I did in life was so I could run," he said about jobs he's chosen.

Phil Pillin, a 55-year-old runner from Ohio with over 135,000 lifetime miles, took advantage of the schedule he had as a high school teacher. He ran twice a day for 40 years, before and after school, plus had summers off. He'd get extra jobs during the summers, but running came first. "Any job I worked, I worked around my running," he said.

Mirth spent his career as a college professor. "I work a lot of hours per week but have a very flexible schedule. So if I want to run at 11:00 in the morning, I can do that. If I want to run at 3:00, I can do that, if I don't have a class. It's been very useful for my running career." Having a job that allows for some flexibility certainly is a boon to running consistently.

Stepping Away from Consistency...and Coming Back

For the purposes of this book, I focused my interviews on runners who have competed continuously from youth to masters, in order to see how they managed each life transition. For them, consistency has been a nonnegotiable since they began running in their teens. But not every successful masters runner fit this pattern precisely. Some picked up the habit later in life, and several started young but then stopped for years, only to rediscover and recommit to the habit later in life.

Ed Whitlock followed this latter pattern. He ran as a teenager in England but then dropped the sport for years, beginning again at age 41. In his early 40s, Whitlock won a World Masters Championship in the 1500 m. After that, he again put running on the back burner until he retired. When he returned to running, he focused on the marathon. In 2016, Whitlock ran a 3:56:34 marathon at age 85. He broke three hours (2:58:40) at age 74 and holds at least 22 single-age world records. Consistent until his death in 2017, he ran up to three hours per day on a small loop in a cemetery near his home. The years off from running do not appear to have detracted from his late success.

Tim Swope, 53, of New York City, was a strong competitor in high school and college. But he quit competing soon after. "It just wore me out," he said of the Division I competitive scene. "Basically, I burned out, got injured."

Following college, Swope's running went from inconsistent to non-existent for two decades. But in his late 40s, Swope discovered that he missed the sport. His son went out for track, and watching him compete, Swope recalled how much fun it had been. He knew he couldn't jump right back in; he had lost so much fitness he could barely run twice around a track.

So he started back slowly, but he still didn't find it easy. "It was probably the most painful process I ever had," he said. "The challenge I had was kick-starting again, getting an old body that had basically been in hibernation state back to running again."

He stuck with it, however, building up the consistency so that today, 40-mile weeks are normal and he does long runs, hills, and an occasional track workout. He's also racing, and with considerable success. He posted a 5:16.68 mile at age 50 and ran a 1:23:11 half-marathon at 51. "I probably enjoy it more than ever," he said.

Burfoot, winner of the 1968 Boston Marathon, put running on the back burner for years. After running 100-plus miles a week for a decade, from 1967 to 1976, he decided it was "time to be a normal person instead of a marathoner," and he cut his miles down to 30 per week.

For two decades, he happily maintained that level, continuing to race but mostly running for the social aspect. "I had fun and didn't care about race results," he said.

His priority in his 30s and 40s was being editor in chief of *Runner's World*. When that role ended, in his late 50s, Burfoot said he had somewhat of a running renaissance. "A lot of responsibility was lifted from my shoulders," Burfoot said. "I decided I might as well do a little bit more running again."

He started training with a local masters group, lost 10 pounds, and started racing better. "I had five to seven years of improving times, of the sort you are supposed to have when you begin running," Burfoot said. He lowered his half-marathon time from around 1:38 to a 1:28 in his early 60s and placed well in his age group in the National Club Cross Country Championships, where he ran on a successful masters team for several years.

Dave Griffin, 56, took his 30s mostly off, just running a bit to keep in shape. He returned in his 40s, partially because his kids were old enough to require less time, but he also found that he had mostly moved beyond comparing his older self to his youthful times. "Enough time had passed that the old history probably wasn't as much an inhibitor," he said.

Taking a break, even if only from competing, can let you start over again, either physically, giving you the opportunity to hone your body and improve again, or emotionally, letting you set new marks untethered from history.

Key to such a comeback, however, is to rebuild your regular training volume and intensity gradually. Whatever your age, you can't just jump back to doing what you did earlier. This is particularly true if you're now over 40.

"Use gradual increases in loads," Gabbett said. "Build to a high-point workload, but try and get there as safely as you can."

Competitive Running versus Competitive Partying

Another runner who's had an on-again, off-again running career, 56-year-old Pete Magill, has been exceptional when he's on, and when he falls off, he has also done so spectacularly. In high school, Magill had moderate success, but after a "respectable but disappointing" cross-country season his senior year, he didn't go out for track the next spring. "My buddies and I decided that instead of sports we would drink beer, and instead of going to college we would go live on an island," he said.

Magill actually did go and live on Saint John in the US Virgin Islands. A few years later, however, he came back to California and got back into running. Competing for Glendale Junior College, he made All-American status and ran the fastest time in the state for the year in the 5000 m. But after graduation, he returned to the Caribbean, where he again drank more than ran.

At 27, he returned again to California. "I remember going back to the track my first day, thinking, *I have got to get my life back or I'm going to drop dead*," he said. "I remember running 3 laps on the track and climbing into the stands and lying there for 30 minutes because

I thought I was going to have a heart attack." That run, however, was the beginning of what he called "an incremental progression—back to health, back to life."

Magill not only got back to health but to being competitive. He ran 30 flat for the 10K, in the 14:30s for the 5K. But it didn't last, due to a burgeoning career. "When I sold my first screenplay in my early 30s, that ended my competitive running and reignited my competitive party lifestyle," he said.

It took a life crisis to bring him back to the sport for good. Working long, late hours trying to crank out 30 pages a day as a screenwriter, he found himself divorced and trying to care for his 6-year-old son. Smoking, drinking, and popping pills to deal with the schedule and stress, he collapsed one night and ended up in the emergency room.

The ER doctor told him he needed to change his lifestyle or he wouldn't live to see his son graduate from high school. Magill took it seriously. "Two months later, on my 39th birthday, I pulled the Nikes out of the closet and ran myself back into shape and a life that was manageable," Magill said. "I gave up the screenwriting and got a job that gave me time to be both a parent and to run."

Magill has run ever since. "My 40s were the happiest times of my life," he said. "I finally had things in balance. If running wasn't the most important thing, it was certainly the catalyst for change and the element of each day that kept me on track."

Reset Breaks

Magill now runs consistently and hard: up to 90-mile weeks and workouts like 20 × 400 m. But he's willing to take breaks. After several years of battling an Achilles problem, he took a full year away from running at age 55 to strengthen and rebuild his body.

This did not mean a year off from fitness, however. He hiked, lifted, and rode an ElliptiGO, a unique cross between an elliptical trainer and a bike that closely mimics the running motion.

"After six years of Achilles bursitis, I had almost given up," he said. He's done this before, reached the end of his rope and thought, *I'm done. I'm never running again.* But each time he thinks this, he finds it frees him to consider a new solution.

"People often keep doing the same thing and having the same problems," Magill explained. "They're scared to stop doing the same thing—because that thing worked for them at some point. They won't stop doing that thing for fear that they'll never get back to where they were before, even though that thing now is not allowing them to get back."

Magill avoids this trap with a mental reboot. "I quit. I accept that what I'm doing isn't working and I can't keep doing it like this," he said. "Once I've accepted that, I can figure out something different. If that works, I'm back in the game," he said, adding, "and thankfully, it has always worked."

After a year off, Magill is back to running and is pain free. "If there is one thing I've learned from being this old, [it's that] there is always a tomorrow," Magill said. "If I had to take a year off in order to have 20 more years on, that wasn't much of a price to pay."

Clearly, consistency is key to lifelong running. But it's important to remember that breaks are not the death of us as runners. In fact, the ability to take breaks may make continuing much more likely.

In *The Power of Habit*, Duhigg also points out that there is a fine line between habit and addiction. Many lifetime runners long ago crossed that line. For the most part, with running the addiction is positive. But it can become a negative addiction if the rewards of the daily run push you out the door when you're hurt or make you push the pace even when you should rest.

The need for rest leads us to the next key for longevity: variety.

KEY 1
CONSISTENCY

- Run often: Even short, easy days maintain the habit and build volume.
- Make running the default option each day: Not if, but when.
- Achieve a tireless state: Run enough mileage so you comfortably finish each run wishing you could run farther.
- Take breaks: A day off, or even three, doesn't make you inconsistent and is often necessary.
- Maintain year-round fitness to avoid injury-producing spikes in training load.

3

VARIETY
MIXING THINGS UP

To every thing there is a season,
and a time to every purpose under the heaven.

−SOLOMON, ECCLESIASTES 3:3 (KJV)

"How many miles do you run every day?" a well-meaning acquaintance asks. I hear that question a lot.

I give the easy answer: "I average about six to eight."

"So you run six miles a day?"

Now I have to elaborate. "No. Some days I run six. Sometimes I'll run 10 or 20. Sometimes only four, but I'll do something faster."

Pause. "But you run every day, right?"

"Sometimes. But I usually take one or two days off every week."

"Oh . . . "

These exchanges often end with a feeling that I've somehow disappointed my friend, that my running isn't quite as serious or impressive as he or she had thought. But though consistency is imperative for lifetime runners, running is not a daily pill doled out in a constant dosage that corresponds to one's level of commitment.

For while lifetime competitors all have impressive life totals and averages from running regularly for many years, they are not what Emerson called "foolishly consistent."

By this I mean they don't run the same distance and pace day after day. They take days off. They take days easy. Some days they run short and fast, and some days they run longer and moderately fast. Some days they go very long and slow the pace considerably. They run on trails, roads, and tracks.

The training of runners who survive through the years
echoes the cycles of nature.

In short, their consistency makes way for the second key to running for life: variety, both daily variety and larger cycles of variety throughout the year. The training of runners who survive through the years echoes the cycles of nature: The sun comes up every day, but the weather is somewhat different from yesterday and considerably different in spring than it was in winter.

ALTERNATING HARD AND EASY RUNNING

All the lifetime competitors I spoke to reported some cycle of variety in their training. Even streakers recognize the need for variety in their running. "Ideally, a veteran streaker gets the maximum benefit from his or her running streak by stirring up the running mix on a constant basis," wrote John Strumsky on the Streak Runners International website. "He or she will—at different times—run hard or race, run easy or jog, run long or run short to properly condition him or herself. A typical week's running schedule might alternate one long run, two or three medium length runs and three or four shorter runs."

The most basic training variety is simply to alternate hard and easy days. Mirth began to pay more attention to this type of cycle after college when, no longer training under a coach, he found that his naturally competitive spirit was driving him to run hard every day. "I went to an exaggerated hard/easy schedule," he said. "So I might be running double workouts of 14 plus 6 miles on one day, with one of those being a pretty hard run. The next day, [I'd do] a really easy 7 to 8 miles."

Like most high-performing runners, Mirth found the hard days to be an easy fit for his competitive personality. It was the easy days that were hard for him to stick to. But he did so steadfastly in order to ensure recovery, and he still does today. To make easy days happen, he adopts an intentionally casual approach. "I just go out, leaving the watch at home," he said. "Just do the miles. I don't care if I'm doing seven minutes or eight minutes or whatever."

He's maintained this alternating schedule for 25 years, and although his paces have slowed, they remain impressive. He believes that variety has been key to his ability to keep running and racing at a high level.

Some lifetime competitors' alternating hard/easy days are more extreme. Olympic marathoner Deena Kastor, describing her training cycle, said, "All of my training was really just grinding and putting in a massive amount of work—and then resting really hard so I can recover and do it again."

Durden credits a hiking accident for his adoption of an alternating hard day/easy day schedule, which he said helped him survive injury as well as improve his performance.

In 1977, he was hiking in the Alps when a rock, kicked loose above him, smashed his knee. Although he could still run on it a bit, the knee hurt every day. He had no intention of stopping his running, so to minimize the pain, Durden adopted an extreme hard/easy program. "I'd run until the knee hurt, then the next day I'd take off," he said. He repeated this pattern for months.

The knee slowly healed, and eventually he started running a 15- to 20-minute slow jog on his easy days. By the end of his recovery period, he was running 2 hours one day and a half hour the next.

Durden continued this alternating schedule, totaling around 90 miles per week throughout the fall of '77. In February of '78, he entered a few races to test the waters and discovered to his surprise that he was winning events he hadn't been able to win before. "I was running faster than I had been able to run," he said. He has no doubt that the hard/easy approach is part of what made the difference.

A VARIETY OF WORKOUTS

In addition to alternating hard days with recovery days, many lifetime competitors structure their training around a weekly cycle, one filled with a variety of workouts. Cycles will often include a long run, one or two different-speed workouts—hills, intervals, or tempo runs—and easy days.

Mirth shared logs detailing his workouts across many years of running (see "John Mirth's Running Logs Across the Decades"). Sample weeks pulled from each of his running decades, from the '80s to today, show not only how he has maintained volume over the years but also reveal the variety in workouts that has kept him race fit—from interval sessions to tempo runs (which he labels "fairly good" pace), hills, and fartleks. Note that in the 2012 excerpt, which shows two consecutive weeks, we see even greater variety as he approached age 50. In addition to alternating hard and easy days, he adopted a pattern of hard/easy weeks: An 86-mile week is followed by a 53-mile week.

Many longtime runners reported similar cycles. They hit multiple speeds regularly, working all their systems and keeping the training varied and interesting.

JOHN MIRTH'S RUNNING LOGS ACROSS THE DECADES

APRIL 1983, AGE: 21

	SUN. 10	MON. 11	TUES. 12	WED. 13	THURS. 14	FRI. 15	SAT. 16	WEEK TOTAL
a.m.	15	5	5	5			11	89
p.m.		10 w/ 2 x 1600 + 2 x 800	11	11 w/ 5 "fairly good"	7	9 w/ 10,000m race		

MAY 1996, AGE: 34

	SUN. 12	MON. 13	TUES. 14	WED. 15	THURS. 16	FRI. 17	SAT. 18	WEEK TOTAL
a.m.	0	15	8	12 w/ 2 x 800 + 33 minutes "fairly good"	8	15 w/ 3 x 1.5m hills	9	82
p.m.		5		5		5		

APRIL 2005, AGE: 43

	SUN. 10	MON. 11	TUES. 12	WED. 13	THURS. 14	FRI. 15	SAT. 16	WEEK TOTAL
a.m.	18	8	12	14 w/ 4 x 600 + 4 x 400	8	13 w/ fartlek 3-4-5-6-6-5-4-4 min.	0	94
p.m.				8	6	7		

APRIL 2012, AGE: 50

	SUN. 1	MON. 2	TUES. 3	WED. 4	THURS. 5	FRI. 6	SAT. 7	WEEK TOTAL
a.m.	20	10	0	5	7	7 w/ 1 mile tempo + 1 mile race pace	9	93
p.m.				15 steady	13	7		

	SUN. 8	MON. 9	TUES. 10	WED. 11	THURS. 12	FRI. 13	SAT. 14	WEEK TOTAL
a.m.	7	13 w/ 4 x 2 mile hill loops	0	0	7	6 w/ 2400 + 1200 + 800 + 400	12	53
p.m.						8		

SEASONAL VARIETY

Variety doesn't stop with daily or weekly cycles. For many runners, these patterns are then wrapped into larger cycles of seasons. Seasons can simply be a buildup to a single peak race, or they can be based on different types of racing. Some runners will do one or two marathon buildups a year, for example, and then race shorter distances at other times of the year. Or they'll change venues, following the patterns of scholastic and pro runners.

Sperandeo, for example, has a track season and a road racing season. "When I have a track season I don't road race, and when I'm road racing I don't do track," he said. He believes training for different distances varies the stress on his body and adds to his longevity.

Kruell adds variety by running a variety of different types of races in spring and summer, such as the Hood to Coast Relay, but focuses her training toward cross-country in the fall and winter. After that season ends, she takes a break.

"I'll take a month or so and do whatever I feel like, just fun," she said. "I give myself permission to run just what I like to."

Kruell doesn't take off completely during these weeks. "I still go out every day. Might be half an hour, might be an hour, or more than an hour," she said. But she doesn't do any workouts or keep track of her running then. "I definitely have weeks when I'm just playing," she said. "I try not to stress too much on those off times about what my mileage is."

Many runners base their schedules on the actual seasons, with winter a time of recovery away from racing, spring and fall full of long races, and summer often peppered with short road events or trail races.

Lull Between Seasons

Seasons also provide the chance for training breaks. Breaks, another type of variety, are a time to back off and recharge runners for the next challenge. Sperandeo takes four planned breaks a year and credits these, at least in part, for his longevity. "If you don't plan a break, a break will be planned for you," he warned.

Breaks, another type of variety, are a time to back off
and recharge runners for the next challenge.

He doesn't stop running completely during a break because, as discussed in Chapter 2, he feels it's too hard to come back from time off and finds it makes injury more likely. Between seasons, he'll take two weeks easy; during that time, he'll get out for short jogs, about 4 miles a day, five days a week. Following two weeks of this kind of recovery, he'll take a few weeks to build back up to his normal 55 or so miles per week.

In addition to these planned breaks, Sperandeo finds that now, in his 50s, he needs mini-breaks midseason. He doesn't plan these breaks but rather takes them when his body tells him he needs to. A few low-energy workouts or difficulty sleeping are typical indicators that he needs to take a break.

Like the planned breaks, his mini-breaks aren't completely off. He'll simply forgo hard workouts and run easy for a week. "Then I get right back in where I should have been, and immediately I'm feeling better," he said.

PERIODIZATION: ORGANIZED VARIETY

Within a season, many runners follow a pattern of periodization. Periodization broadly refers to the process of working different systems at different times as you progress toward a competitive goal.

Coates believes that methods he learned from legendary coach Arthur Lydiard have helped him stay largely injury free. Following Lydiard, he builds his capacity in training periods that differ from one another and ascend to a season peak. Coates doesn't believe the periods have to be in the same order as Lydiard dictates; he thinks that you can play around with them. Others debate this vigorously. Proper ordering of the periods is an area where people can get religiously strict, and there isn't science to confirm definitively what the "right" order should be, or even what type of training each should contain. For most, it's a matter of feeling things out to discover what works best.

Regardless of the order of the periods, the key idea is that you don't do everything at the same time. At one stage, you stress speed, at another, strength. Sometimes you build endurance. You're always training, but you're training different systems. You create variety within your consistency.

RUNNING OF THE FAST VARIETY

When preparing for a race, running fast is essential. You need to train fast to race fast, and if you want to race your best, you need to improve different systems: lactate threshold, VO_2max, and max turnover.

While all this is true, lifetime competitors repeatedly revealed that they don't run fast just to prep for a race—they run fast some days simply because they enjoy it.

Rodgers does up-tempo repeats at different venues around Boston, on a bike path or a dirt road alongside the Charles. "I've always done some training. I still like to," Rodgers said about his speed work.

He described the joy of racing a friend in his fast workouts. His buddy is 10 years younger and gives Rodgers a head start. "Then he chases me. As soon as I hear him, I'll just move enough quicker," he said, pumping his arms with glee. "Sometimes you get caught—you get nailed. You're having fun. Doesn't really matter your age." Rodgers laughed and his eyes lit up; he was clearly relishing the joy of running hard.

When Kastor moved into the masters ranks, she tried moderating her workouts, running at controlled paces rather than pushing the limits.

She found that this didn't excite her like running hard did, and so she went back to an intense hard/easy schedule.

She prefers the feeling of red-lining it, whatever that pace may be. She runs her easy days easy so she can take her hard days even harder, she said. "I'm very good at taking easy days—but those hard days are intense, and I love that."

THE JOYS OF VARIETY

Some competitors have given up racing as they've grown older, yet they still do the variety work necessary to keep seriously fit.

Grimes once made his living as a road runner. Today, he still cares how fast he can run, but he rarely races. That doesn't keep him from running a variety of different paces and workouts.

"Doing the work to get into really good shape—it's like trying to touch that spark of the divine," Grimes said. "It's all about getting out there every day and enjoying the process."

Process is a topic Grimes returned to repeatedly as he talked about his changing relationship to the sport. "If you enjoy the process, when you get in shape, part of the process is to run hard," he said. "That is part of the enjoyment. There's nothing better than climbing a monstrous hill that's harder than hell to get to the top and making it, and turning around and looking at what you've done."

For Grimes, the daily run is the point, not the race. But contrary to conventional wisdom that equates easy with fun, Grimes has to go hard to enjoy the full spectrum of the daily run. A full running life is much more than running easy all the time, he insisted.

Douglas, like Grimes, no longer feels moved to race. You wouldn't know it by his training schedule, however. He still runs more than 60 miles per week and does all the things people who race do to prepare for racing.

"I do what people would think of as training," Douglas said. "I do long runs. I do turnover work. I do drills."

Like Grimes, Douglas appreciates different types of running for their own sake. "I enjoy the variety; I like the process," Douglas said. "It feels good. There are times when it simply feels good to run fast. There are times when it feels great to absolutely crawl."

Douglas concedes that it might look silly to some that he puts on racing shoes, does fast workouts, drills, and striders, yet almost never races. But he sees it differently—the variety is not a means to another end but a key part of what makes running enjoyable. "I don't have the same thing for dinner every night. I don't want to read the same thing all the time. Why wouldn't I want to do different things?"

=

WHY IT MATTERS

Variety might be enjoyable for its own sake, but it's also essential to longevity for several reasons.

The first reason stems from the way training works. You get stronger by stressing the body then giving it time to recover. After recovering back to the baseline level, the body reacts to the stress by making itself stronger so it can be better prepared for such a stress the next time. This improvement process, called supercompensation, actually occurs during recovery.

"In supercompensation, the athlete can handle the same training load or a greater load with ease in the subsequent workouts if recovery is adequate and the new stress is timed properly," Vern Gambetta explained in his book *Athletic Development*. "The training volume, intensity, and frequency must be appropriate for the particular athlete."

If training is too intense, the athlete will struggle to get back to baseline and no supercompensation will occur. Thus, the process of physical training, by nature, requires the ups and downs of stress and recovery. Some athletes can recover in 24 hours, but most require a longer recovery period, which, Gambetta said, "can be a lighter training session, a recovery session, or active rest"—in other words, an easy day or even an off day.

Not only is this important for conditioning, it also keeps you from getting injured. Runners quickly discover that an all hard/all the time schedule lands them on the disabled list. Research bears this out. A 2014 study out of San Diego State University looked at the summer training of 463,000 high school cross-country runners and concluded that those who did not vary their mileage on different days were at higher risk for injury.

Working It All

A second reason for variety is the need to stress multiple systems. To compete well in a distance race, you need to have every aspect of the running body firing on all cylinders. Since different intensities of training work different physiological systems, you must vary your pace to hit each system. Long runs build endurance, short sprints spur your neuromuscular system, long intervals increase your maximal oxygen uptake, and tempo runs improve your lactate threshold.

Coates embraces variety for this reason. But he finds that many runners are too tied to one thing. During the early days of *Runner's World*, Coates would go out with a training group at lunch. After a while, some of the guys told him they would no longer train with him because he went too slow. Ironically, those same guys had marathon PRs 10 or more minutes slower than Coates. He'd just smile and say, "There are days I run fast and days I run slow."

He believes in variety, both on daily runs and in workouts. And he's not alone. Across the board, lifetime competitors, even those in their

50s, 60s, and beyond, add fast speed work to their running. Joe Friel argues in his book *Fast After 50* that "intensity, not duration, is the key to high performance in experienced athletes." He cites research that shows we lose more in terms of performance as we age if we neglect the intense work, even if we maintain endurance.

In addition to the variety of paces in their distance workouts, successful distance runners at any age also do some runs at full speed to work their explosive muscles and neuromuscular systems. Brad Hudson, top running coach and author of *Run Faster*, advocates doing short hill sprints regularly, even if you are a marathoner. "It's like opening up a fire hose to full blast," said Hudson.

I've watched Kenyan distance runners do "diagonals"—repeated sprints from corner to corner of a soccer field—as part of their daily warm-up. Some sort of "striders" are important for every runner to get full range of motion and recruit every muscle and nerve.

The need for these doesn't stop as you age. Emery, age 70, with 50 years of competitive running on her legs, sprints at the end of every run. Roger Robinson, who still trains and races at age 77, says that while the specifics of his fast workouts may have changed over the years, he still does them faithfully, with sessions such as 15 × 1 minute and 10 × 2 minutes.

How to combine different paces and what the "best" workouts look like—be they pickups during a run or timed intervals, on a track or on muddy hills—are the topics of many articles and books. These patterns and combinations differ for each lifetime competitor. In interviews, most emphasized that everyone needs to find his or her own pattern rather than try to follow someone else's. Several cited George Sheehan's quote about being "an experiment of one." Coates said, "The best method is the one that works for you."

Mostly Easy

One consistent element of training among successful longtime runners is that their up-tempo workouts make up only a small part of the full volume of their running. Researchers have observed that the majority of top performers only run faster than their ventilatory threshold (or tempo pace), during 20 percent of their running or less. They do 80-plus percent of their running at easy, less intense efforts. Matt Fitzgerald details this research and its implications in his book *80/20 Running*.

The 80/20 ratio also highlights a need for our key from Chapter 2, consistency, as you must run a considerable amount at lower intensities to balance even a small amount of harder effort.

While specific ratios vary, generally speaking, all lifetime competitors seemed to do a small amount of intense work relative to the volume of running easy. For most, as they age, both the volume of hard runs and long runs goes down, keeping the ratio of hard to easy runs similar to what they did in their youth.

Spreading the Stress

Along with their belief that variety is part of a full running life, several lifetime competitors felt that it also helps keep them off the injured list, another reason that variety is key. "I fully believe that the variety, rather than being a potential source of injury, is a prophylactic against injury," Douglas said.

Sports med doctors support this claim. Rob Conenello, DPM, a sports podiatrist, runner, and form expert, says that doing the same thing over and over is the definition of overuse and causes injury.

"We need more variability. That's the spice of life," Conenello told me. He points to kids, who naturally race across the playground or chase each other in tag. Their pace changes constantly. In contrast, when they start running for conditioning, they're told to trudge along at a constant pace. As they get older, they keep trudging at that same pace every day, which leads to overuse injuries, he said.

Some runners I interviewed felt variety can actually replace stretching and other flexibility work. Robinson doesn't believe in supplemental work, without apology. He articulated his position about stretching and running variety best in a 2004 *Running Times* article:

> *The flexibility a runner needs is running specific. You get it by making your running varied and natural. Instead of bashing every mile on the same unyielding blacktop or concrete road surface, run on trails and tracks, hills and hollows, soggy mud, sticky clay, and springy grass, splash through puddles and skitter over stones and struggle through sand—whatever you can find that is varied and natural. Running at speed for a long time over all kinds of terrain is how people two million years ago used to do the grocery shopping. It stretches everything that needs stretching for running, and, more importantly, it works everything, too.*

Research is slim in this area, but John Kiely, senior lecturer in elite performance at the Institute of Coaching and Performance, University of Central Lancashire, UK, says that what research we have hints at the larger picture that we know from practice. Kiely researches neural plasticity, the ability of the body to adapt to new patterns and then form efficient pathways. Variety, he said, is essential in this process of rewiring; runners need variety to keep their stride fresh and optimal, particularly after injury or when working on improving mechanics.

Kiely points out that there is enough research to suggest that "elevated training monotony—which may be broadly perceived as a lack of variation—leads to increased incidence of overtraining syndromes." In other words, monotony not only can bore you, it can hurt you.

A recent project out of the University of Wisconsin hints at this relationship between variety of training and injury prevention. The study showed that high school athletes who specialized in one sport were twice as likely to suffer injury. While lifetime runners tend to stick with one sport, the key variable here is a variety of training stresses. Variety of stress can also be accomplished by varying running patterns. Another study links reduced injury risk to running in a variety of shoes, which subtly alters your stride patterns and stresses.

Even if science hasn't definitively proven the relationship between variety and reduced injury, evidence certainly points to variety helping. Since it also makes you a better runner and it's fun, it seems like an excellent idea to mix training up.

WHAT SHOULD I DO TODAY?

Building variety within consistency is simple: Run regularly, but at different distances and intensities. Channeling food writer Michael Pollan, I once wrote that the key to running well is to "Run often. At different paces. Mostly easy."

At its most simple level, introducing variety lets you have fun. So find your inner child and just haul once in a while.

But remember, the top end is only part of the equation; many runners run too fast too much of the time. Their daily pace is essentially as fast as they can manage without focusing, neither all out nor easy. Coaches like Hudson say it is much better to have constant, huge variation in your training, both very fast and very slow.

To run slow enough to provide the bottom end of that variety, you may need to check your ego. Many runners want to maintain an image of themselves within the pecking order and so are unwilling to run slow enough to recover. The antidote is to have confidence in who you are and not need affirmation of your speed every time out. This requires a strong, healthy running identity.

Beyond Habit to Identity

Creating that strong running identity helps you deal with another problem that crops up when variety is introduced into consistency: Changing things up, such as taking days off or running at different times and venues, can make forming the all-important running habit harder.

In *The Power of Habit*, Duhigg points out that habits can be fragile—a change in the cue can short-circuit the pattern and eliminate the routine. You may not be able to let the habit take over if you don't run the exact same script day after day. The need for variety adds questions—How far? How fast?—to the decision, which drops you out of the automatic loop and can lead to questioning whether to get out at all.

One of the keys to maintaining a continuity that is more robust than a habit is the formation of a running identity. Psychologist Erik Erikson considered the formation of identity a central task of the individual, and particularly important in adolescence. In *Identity and the Life Cycle*, Erikson defined the identity as "a successful alignment of the individual's *basic drives* with his *endowment* and his *opportunities*."

You find yourself when what you *want to do* agrees with what you are *able to do* and what you have the *chances to do*. That sounds a lot like the stories I heard from runner after runner about their adolescent experience: finding in running something that they could compete at and have success in, and then learning to love it and wanting to continue to do it.

Erikson goes on to talk about identity in terms of "one's ability to maintain inner sameness and continuity" and how this helps us deal with subsequent life crises and changes. Knowing who we are in one area helps us weather times when other parts of our identity crumble.

My experience is similar to others in that crises often drove me deeper into running. When in college I broke up with a girlfriend, for example, I coped by going for long, hard runs. Three lifetime competitors told me their best training came during or after a divorce. When challenging outside circumstances forced me to change my profession, what did I do first? I started training for a marathon. Being a runner, and being able to maintain and control that, provides continuity of identity.

I'm a Runner

Writing on people's passion for activities, psychologist Robert Vallerand of the University of Quebec at Montreal noted, "Such passions become central features of one's identity and serve to define the person. Those who have a passion for playing the guitar, for reading, or for jogging do not merely play the guitar, read, or jog. They are 'guitar players,' 'readers,' or 'joggers.' Passionate activities are part of who they are."

I discovered that this held true for every lifetime competitor I talked to. To a person, each viewed him- or herself not as someone who runs but as a runner. Running is a major part of their personal identity.

When asked if it ever had entered his mind to hang up his shoes, for example, Dunham responded, "Never. This is what I do. I've known since sometime in high school. When people say, 'This is Dave, he's a runner,' you become that. That's how I define myself. First and foremost."

Sperandeo said he knew early who he was. "When you're in your 20s and you have a group of running friends, you know most are not going to always compete," he said. "There's just one or two that you know are runners. I was one of those." Running is so ingrained, Sperandeo continued, that even when he tried to quit it a few times, he simply could not.

Built, Not Born

Contrary to those who talk about not being a "true" runner because they aren't good enough, running identity doesn't seem to depend on ability for lifetime competitors. As I learned while researching this book, most lifetime competitors weren't that good at the start or didn't see themselves as that good. But they loved to run, did it often, and built their ability. And in doing so, they and others came to see themselves as runners.

Identity helps to maintain consistency even when you include variety, because it doesn't require a cue to set it into motion, as a habit does. If you see yourself as a runner, you'll make the time to run sometime in your day, even when schedules throw off your patterns.

Having a strong running identity helps you to take breaks as well. Knowing you are a runner gives you the confidence to not have to reassure yourself of your status every day.

"Some people don't have the confidence to take breaks," Sperandeo said. "If you have a bad workout, don't think the sky has fallen. You have to have the confidence to rest when you need it."

This kind of confidence also provides a resistance against the pressure of the "miles per day" or "miles per week" questions. Too often we'll sacrifice variety for impressive volume and fail to hit peaks because we're not willing to go through the rest and downtime valleys. A habit to run consistently combined with an identity confident enough to build variety into that consistency is a powerful combination that builds successful and resilient runners.

KEY 2
VARIETY

- Take time to get stronger: Alternate hard and easy training to produce the stress and recovery cycles necessary to build strength and fitness.
- Work every system: Run at a variety of paces to develop all aspects of your running body.
- Spice it up: Mix up your pace, terrain, and routine regularly to keep it interesting and build injury-resistant strength and mobility.
- Know who you are: Maintain your running habit despite shaking up your routine by fostering a strong identity as a runner who doesn't need daily affirmation.

4

TRAINING BY FEEL
LETTING GO OF THE WATCH AND SCHEDULE

Age isn't how old you are but how old you feel.

–GABRIEL GARCÍA MÁRQUEZ

As runners, we crave details on how to maximize our time and efforts: How many miles should we run, how many repeats, what pace on which runs on which days? Charts and numbers fill training books and magazine articles. We download training apps that tell us exactly what we should be doing each day. The market is saturated with devices that allow us to track every number, every step.

But what if a key to both achieving your best and staying in the race is to stop planning and tracking? What if instead, you just listened to your body and ran how you felt?

SEAT OF MY PANTS

"Sorry about being late," Joan Benoit Samuelson said when she phoned midafternoon on a January weekday. She had promised to call that morning to follow up with details about her 60th birthday marathon celebration. She didn't need to apologize—the first lady of American running is busy, active, and engaged, with a demanding schedule. The reason she was late, however, caught my interest. "I ended up doing a long run," she said. "The weather was beautiful, the roads were dry, so I went 20."

Benoit Samuelson's impromptu long run perfectly illustrates her philosophy of running how she feels on any given day. "I always went by the seat of my pants," Benoit Samuelson told me a month earlier while sipping a latte at a coffee shop in Freeport, Maine. "I still do, I always did, run the way I felt."

Benoit Samuelson is an accomplished lifetime competitor. She's won gold medals and set world records, and has continued to compete and set age-group records throughout her running career, right up to the present.

That she runs by feel grabbed my attention. And it turns out, she wasn't the only one.

When I started interviewing lifetime competitors, I expected that most, to achieve their high level of success, would have followed carefully prepared plans, aimed for weekly mileage goals, clicked off specific splits during specific workouts, and could detail exactly how they adjusted those totals and times as they aged. I imagined finding boxes full of training logs where the workouts and totals had accumulated and there discover formulas to guide runners through the decades.

And I did find some of that. But far more often, I discovered that those who keep going at a high level, such as Benoit Samuelson, train more by feel than by plan and consider it an important element in their success and longevity.

Within this shared propensity, however, I discovered lots of variability. At one end of the spectrum were those with almost no structure to their training at all, and at the other end were the planners who use feel only as a final test of their performance.

DOING ONLY WHAT SHE LIKES

The most unstructured runner I met was Roxi Erickson of Omaha. Erickson, 54, has a marathon PR of 2:39:25 and was known for racing, and winning, multiple marathons in a year, often once a month.

Erickson has never had an injury that kept her from running, and throughout decades of competing, her passion for the sport has never waned. She credits this to an innate love for the sport coupled with her unconventional training, which, in a nutshell, amounted to running every day at whatever pace and distance she felt like.

"When I ran marathons," Erickson said. "I never had one of those things that said I should be tapering or I should being running this this day and this the next day." (She's so far removed from structured training that she doesn't know what to call a training plan.) "People say, 'Oh, it says I'm supposed to run 18 miles today.' I could never do that," she said. "If I don't feel like running 18 miles, I'm not going to be able to go do it. I've always run how I feel."

When running was her full-time job, she would do speed workouts with a group, which meant she had at least one day's workout formally scheduled. Since becoming a schoolteacher, however, she's reverted to just getting out daily and running at whatever pace feels good. While she used to go out for an hour or more each day, lately she finds she's usually doing a morning run of 35 to 55 minutes—"depends on what I feel like"— and 60 to 75 minutes on weekends. Off that training, she's still able to run 5Ks in the 21- to 22-minute range.

Erickson is at one extreme end on the run-by-feel spectrum, someone who loves to run and run hard, and simply does that, without plan or measurement. She knows herself and has been doing this long enough that she can get race ready and avoid injury by following her instincts.

This may be the ideal, but few are able or willing to leave quite so much to emotion and sensation.

COOKING WITHOUT A BOOK

A small step along the spectrum toward more structured training is to let feel dictate what you do from among a range of options, or, as Gary Allen sees it, ingredients.

Allen, now 60, of Great Cranberry Island, Maine, started running in high school in 1972 at 15 and never stopped. He's now run 101 marathons, 68 of them under three hours.

Allen eschews rigid training plans. He credits his longevity and lack of injuries to what he calls "learning how to be a chef."

"My training has always been unconventional," he told me over breakfast in Millinocket, Maine. Never at a loss for words, Allen spoke at length, wrapping his experience in colorful metaphors and encompassing philosophies.

When it comes to cooking, he says, many people follow a cookbook and try to get everything exact. "Exactly 2/3 of a cup of flour. Next, a teaspoon of butter. They have to get it exact, or it won't work. A lot of runners run like they are following a recipe. Whereas a lot of people who become chefs cook by instinct."

Allen believes runners should do more than just follow a recipe; they should be chefs. It's a process that takes some work. He learned to be a chef, he says, by studying numerous training philosophies and distilling the basic ingredients common to all of them. From that point, he is able to combine them according to taste. He thinks others can and should do the same. "Become a chef and stop following the recipe," Allen said. "Get those basic ingredients in your mix, and the order you put them in there is less important."

In practice, this means doing whatever feels right to him on any given day, all the while making sure he regularly gets in a variety of types of runs (another key habit, examined in Chapter 3). When training for a marathon, for example, he makes sure he gets in a long run every week to 10 days. But he does not schedule it for a certain day. "A lot of times, it would be a spontaneous thing: In your mind you're thinking, *I'm going to do eight or so*, but you'd feel so good at eight, you'd keep going for a 22-miler," he said, echoing Benoit Samuelson.

The same holds true for speed days. "On days when your stride is light and quick, those would turn into fartlek days," he said. That fartlek could be to repeat half miles or push the hills or do a tempo run; he lets his body guide him to what feels best. Allen doesn't time his runs or use a GPS watch. He trusts his internal monitoring to know what is the appropriate effort for each type of run.

Become a chef and stop following the recipe. Get those basic ingredients in your mix, and the order you put them in there is less important.
                                            –GARY ALLEN

"A lot of times, I'd design a workout as I went," Allen said. "I would just go out running with an open, empty mind. Does an artist know what he is going to paint before he paints it?"

Allen isn't the only lifetime competitor who has adopted an open "how-do-I-feel-today" approach. Kartalia, who followed more structured training when he was young and training to make the Olympic Trials 10,000 m, relaxed his approach after turning 40.

"I do hard workouts, but not on a rigid schedule," Kartalia said. "Most days, I don't even know what I'm going to do until I'm 2 miles into my run. If I feel great, I'll get rolling or I'll go to the track and do some intervals, or go to a hill and do some repeats. The days when I feel so-so or bad, I'll adjust accordingly, in the run." Kartalia lets his body dictate when to back off as well. "If I feel a very low motivation for a week, I'll take a break," he said. "I'll run five to six days, 3 to 4 miles, a big drop. I'll bounce thinking like, 'Yeah, I needed that.'"

To be this kind of chef, or artist, requires a keen self-awareness and focus. "The trick is to identify what is going on with your body," Allen said. "Once you get that clarity, then you can quickly identify what kind of run it is going to be."

PLAYING WITH THE INGREDIENTS

Allen's approach wasn't always so free. As a young marathoner, he tried running 140 miles per week when he heard that was what Bill Rodgers did. But he found that he got tired instead of fit, and he concluded that such a high volume of training was too much for him.

During another significant early year, he resolved to build up to 70 miles per week. He started in January, running 3 miles per day, seven days a week. Every month he added another daily mile, building the habit and the strength and endurance foundation to handle the volume. By July, he was doing 10 miles per day, every day.

For years afterward, he ran a consistent 70 miles per week. "I made it something you don't think about, like brushing your teeth," he said. Out of this habit, his training eventually morphed into something less regimented: "Doing 6 easy here and 12 hard there, and getting the basic ingredients in."

Even now, while he's adamant about following his body, he hinted at an underlying discipline. After a day when he feels good and runs a set of hard intervals, for example, he said, "The next day, you might be sore, but you go out religiously, clear your mind—and loping along easily feels good."

To be a chef like Allen takes experimenting and experience. Before you can listen to your body to tell you how far and fast you should run, it helps to have established religious consistency and gathered considerable self-knowledge. Once you have those tools, however, you can relish the freedom of doing what feels right without losing fitness.

A ROUGH PLAN, BUT FEELING THE PACE

Benoit Samuelson's training patterns represent another step along the run-by-feel continuum. She maintained that she's never stuck to a strict schedule—she will sometimes seize the day and go long, as she had the day she called—but she usually has a rough plan in mind. Of her approach to training through the years, she said, "I had an idea of what I wanted to accomplish in a week, when my long run would be, when I'd do a speed workout, that sort of thing."

Running Tide, which she wrote in 1987, offers clues to how she combined planning with adapting. Usually she knew how far she wanted to run on a given day, and then she always made sure she finished it. "If I go out on a twenty-mile loop accepting the idea beforehand that I'm tired and may have to run fifteen, that's okay," she wrote. "But once I've decided how much I can accomplish, I won't do less under any but extraordinary circumstances. I may run more than I planned, but seldom less."

She's also always had a mileage goal for the week. Even when a recent injury caused her to back off that goal and "catch what I can," she admitted that the goal always hovered in the back of her mind.

As for scheduling speed work, she used to go to the track once a week and occasionally train with other elite women. But for the last several years, she simply fits speed into other runs when she's feeling fast. "I try to do pickups, and sometimes I race cars," she said.

Benoit Samuelson's training schedule has grown even more variable as she ages and relaxes. But what has remained true across the decades is that she listens to her body, not the clock, to control her effort.

As for pace, she runs at the one that feels right that day. If she sets out on a long run, for example, she does the run at whatever pace feels good, taking note of the time only after the run to assess how it went. The same goes for speed work. If she feels great, she will run fast, if not, she'll go slow. (Recognize, however, that how Benoit Samuelson feels is usually fast. "My philosophy has always been, 'When in doubt, run harder,'" she said.)

Consistency, our first key habit, pops up too. "I have to run every day. If I don't run, I feel guilty," Benoit Samuelson told a reporter when she was still in high school.

To have the success Benoit Samuelson has had and continues to have, you obviously have to run often, long and hard. But her "seat of my pants" flexibility with pace, paying attention to her body rather than the clock, has certainly been a key part of what's led to her exceptional longevity in the sport.

MIND THE PLAN, BUT DON'T STRESS THE SPLITS

Like Benoit Samuelson, Olympian Colleen De Reuck, 53, lets feel dictate each day's effort level. "You need to have feel," De Reuck told me, sitting at her kitchen table in her home on the north edge of Boulder, Colorado. "Some days you feel good, and others days you don't feel as great."

Unlike Benoit Samuelson, however, she keeps more strictly to a training schedule, following workouts that her coach (and husband) plans for their running club. She won't indulge in more miles at whim. "I'm not going to add anything on, because my whole schedule is planned toward the race," she said. "I'm not going to add to a 20-miler this week if next week I have to do a 20-miler."

But even when a workout is structured and on a track, De Reuck said she doesn't set goal times, but rather, goes by effort. Tuesday workouts are normally something short and fast, going as hard as she can to complete the workout. Fridays are tempo days, also by effort, albeit a more controlled effort.

How does she know exactly how hard to go? De Reuck chalks that up to experience and feels that one key is not stressing too much over hitting exact times. If she's doing a workout that calls for sections at 10K or half-marathon pace, for example, she aims for close to those marks but doesn't obsess over every split. "As you become familiar with your body and your speed, you know that," she said. "It's not an exact pace, but you know where you are at."

In the same vein, when she coaches, she teaches her athletes to judge their efforts internally. She'll give them an idea of an appropriate pace based on race times, but she emphasizes to them that they should be most concerned that the overall *trends* are appropriate. In a progression workout, for example, rather than stressing that they run each segment within a specific range, she emphasizes that each should be faster than the one before it. In her thinking, the process of learning to feel the effort and pace is more important than hitting predetermined splits.

THE DATA KEEPERS

At the most structured end of the spectrum are those who plan workouts and set times based on recent races. Those with this approach tend to race often and keep detailed data of their performances.

New England trail and mountain specialist Dunham said that while he bases his daily pace on effort and avoids looking at his Garmin during runs, he definitely wants to know all the parameters in advance when he does a speed workout. "I prefer to know exactly what I'm doing," he said.

Dunham knows the paces are going to be slower now, at 52, than they were in his 20s, when he ran a 2:19 marathon. But he's able to set exact target paces because he races 30 to 50 times a year and keeps meticulous logs of every result.

Armed with this data, he can judge what workout pace is appropriate. He'll base a session of repeat 800s, for example, on a recent 5K. "I'm very dialed in to what kind of shape I'm in," he said. "I'm good at predicting race times based on my training and then figuring out a workout based on my race times."

Similar sentiments were expressed by other data-driven athletes.

"I'm very time oriented. I'm checking splits. I log everything," said Sonja Friend-Uhl, who, now age 46, has been winning races and setting records since high school in races from the mile to the marathon.

Like Dunham, Friend-Uhl said she is able to base her workouts on times because of her frequent racing and the data it supplies. "I'll run cross, I'll run road, I run indoor and outdoor. So I have a lot of data in front of me, and I can analyze that," she said.

Friend-Uhl uses time goals to pace both speed and tempo runs, and she likes the data because it is empirical, not subject to interpretation. The data lets her know if she's had a good workout. If she doesn't hit her marks, she said, "I know that I'm either being lazy, not tough enough, or something is off."

This last concession is the only place "feel" enters the data keeper's training. Knowing whether a slower time is due to lack of mental toughness or illness requires an analysis of effort. If Friend-Uhl is pushing as hard as she can and still misses the marks, then something must be off and she'll give herself a break.

The data provides the incentive to consider if she is slacking off mentally or if a slow performance is due to something physical. If she were to base this assessment only by feel, she believes it could be too easy to justify a less-than-maximal effort.

POWERED BY PRECISION

In *Fast After 50*, Joe Friel makes the argument that perception, or "feel," has merit, but it's too imprecise to be relied upon. He maintains, "That which is measured improves." A scientist and coach, Friel advocates frequent testing, either through all-out timed efforts or, ideally, in a lab setting, to know your thresholds and maximum capacities by which you can benchmark your efforts by pace or power.

For some, this kind of testing and measuring provides too much structure and stress. It seems that whether you judge workouts by effort or numbers depends on your ability, real or perceived, to assess your efforts accurately, and on your willingness to race frequently or conduct data-collecting tests.

The majority of lifelong runners I interviewed lean toward training by feel, perhaps because they have years of experience or because they want to keep their running simple after all those years. Some, however, find comfort in the numbers, which they must frequently adjust to their current ability.

TECH WARY

A "go-by-feel" approach seems at odds with today's desire to track everything with technology. These days, most runners head out the door with a GPS watch or phone app that times and reports on every mile, even giving real-time pace.

The lifetime competitors I interviewed started running before most of this technology was widely available. And a surprising number of them have eschewed adopting the new technologies along the way. Many don't wear a watch at all. Others simply time known loops with an old-fashioned stopwatch, which gives them their pace after the fact but doesn't interfere with running by effort.

Benoit Samuelson is wary of tech. "I got the new Nike+ watch and ran myself into an injury because I was trying to beat the clock," Benoit Samuelson said. She had to take an uncharacteristic 10 days off. "So I just decided to put that away," she said. A few weeks later, however, she started to use the watch again, but with mixed feelings. While she finds some of the information handy, she doesn't think it's a perfect tool, noting for example that it doesn't take into account the different efforts from changing conditions, like the difference between one morning's run on clear roads with perfect temps and one on snow-covered roads with screws in her shoes. So she continues to depend largely on how she feels.

De Reuck expressed similar hesitations about GPS devices. She likes the ability to see what pace corresponds to a certain effort but fears being too tied to the numbers or, worse, being encouraged to pick up the pace even when her body is telling her no. She believes if you're going slower than your effort would seem to indicate, there's a reason. "Your heart rate and body are telling you you're either coming down with something or you've trained hard, you need to recover," she said. "So don't worry about your Garmin pace; you need to run how you feel."

Similarly, in a race, she warns about trying to hold to a predetermined pace. "If you go to a race, sometimes for no reason—you've done the training, you've done the taper, and it's just not there—you can't force it," she said. "If you start too hard, you'll dig an even bigger hole for yourself." The pressure to hold a pace that doesn't feel right can cause you to crash and burn in the race, she said. She advocates paying more attention to your body than to the watch on race day.

WHY IT MATTERS

Let's face it, no one likes watching race times slow, but it is an inescapable part of growing older. Runner after runner mourns, "I used to run marathons at XX pace, and now I can barely keep that pace up for a 5K!" Focus on this for too long and you might be tempted to hang up your running shoes altogether.

Now, imagine the gift of not noticing your slowing times (or aging body). How is this possible? A wonderful benefit of effort-based training is its ability to let older runners experience running the same way they did 20, 30, or 40 years ago.

Feels Like Old Times

Tuning in to effort allows runners to get the same joy and to feel the same sensations of fitness, power, and speed today as they did when they were younger and faster, regardless of the actual pace they are running.

Fifty-four-year-old middle-distance specialist David Bailey of Iowa finds this feeling on a training loop that he says makes him feel like a kid again. In season, when sharpening for races, he bases his track workouts on race times and his log. There, his slowing paces are easy to see, unfortunately. The rest of the year, however, his workouts are effort based, mostly short, hilly loops on the cinder paths of a local cemetery.

He doesn't aim for a specific time on these loops but rather just runs them as hard as he can. Year after year, he continues to run that same loop. And while he knows intellectually that his times are slowing, what is key is that it never *feels* any different. Regardless of time or pace, the sensation is the same as ever. "You're moving along, the wind's in your hair," he said. "If you don't compare, you get the same sensation."

Mirth echoed these sentiments. He says that while his times have slowed over the years, his effort-based track workouts feel the same today as they ever did. "The thing about 400 workouts, you run as fast as you can," he said. In college, that meant low 60s. Over the decades, he has slowed so that now, in his 50s, he's hitting 75 to 80 seconds. But the specific time doesn't matter, he finds, if he focuses on effort, not his watch.

"My brain doesn't get discouraged by the fact that I'm running 10 seconds slower than I used to," he said. "It still feels fast, because it is hard. So it kind of tricks me into thinking that I'm still pretty fast."

This effect is even greater during workouts where both volume and intensity are effort based. Mirth has had to modify the distance and number of repeats of his track workouts as he's aged, but for fartleks, it's as if nothing has changed. One of his favorite workouts is a ladder working up from 3 minutes to 6 minutes hard, then back down. He doesn't measure his pace or distance, so he's not comparing to old marks. In terms of feel, little has changed since his college days, 30 years ago. "My legs feel pretty wobbly at the end, so I feel like I've done good work, and I get a post-run high and all that good stuff," he said.

Free and Open

Effort-based training not only lets you feel the same, it also reduces the stress of having to perform and live up to expectations and goals every day. Many lifetime competitors welcome this relaxing of daily pressure.

De Reuck prefers fartleks to doing workouts on the track for this reason. "I find a lot of pressure, if you're going to do track work, and you're doing half-mile repeats, and you've got to get them on the time," she said. "I'd rather just go 3 minutes on the trail or the bike paths and run on my efforts."

Allen agreed. Tying yourself to a schedule, he says, sometimes sets you up to fail. "If the schedule says 10 × 800 in under 2:30 and you don't hit that, you've set up a failure point, you didn't do well," he said. "Whereas if I'm running on a Thursday and my legs are clicking, this feels effortless—and suddenly I do 10 × 800 in a run, it is like a gift, it is a success point."

Besides forcing you to continually meet daily tests, Allen notes another problem he finds with schedules. "I think people get a little too caught up," he said. Following all the details, he says, can be overwhelming and even discouraging. "I think it contributes to people having a shorter running career, because it becomes so consuming."

Kartalia agrees that runners can become too obsessed, too structured and strict in their training, reading all the books, buying all the gear, monitoring every heart rate and step. He feels fortunate to have been able to stay clear of this. "I have guidelines in my head," he said. "I want to run most days. I want to run hard on some of those days." But that's about as structured as things get.

He thinks this has been significant in keeping him in the sport and passionate about it. "This has helped me avoid having running seem like a chore, something I had to check off a list," he said. "I did it when I felt like it—which was almost all the time—but I didn't feel like I had to follow super rigid guidelines."

Kartalia has seen others burn out and experienced it some in his youth. His post-40 run-what-you-feel method keeps him burning hot but not burnt out.

"I love the way I run now," he said. "I'm trying to stay at a reasonable level of fitness and competitiveness, but I'm emphasizing [that] above all, I want to enjoy this. I think a happy runner is a better runner."

Kruell agreed. At 58, she says the vast majority of her workouts these days are effort based. She likes how this allows her to keep her training flexible in terms of time and location, and also says it relaxes workouts and keeps her from going too hard. "You don't get all wigged out if you're 2 seconds slower," she said.

But the biggest reason she's drifted toward effort-based training as she's aged is because it takes away the constant comparisons. "You're happier. You're not getting the bad feedback: Oh God, it's so much slower!" Kruell said. "You're relieved of that. You can run hard simply to run hard. Because it is fun. You don't have to hit that particular time to make yourself feel good about it."

For De Reuck, avoiding the clock is a coping strategy for the difficult transition away from not winning races and setting PRs. "Training and racing, the mental part is a huge part of it. If you're going to keep beating yourself up that you're not getting the times, it is just making training hard and unpleasant," she said. "I just go out how I feel; I go run. It is more free and open."

Many other lifetime competitors said they steered clear of watches and logbooks and judged their running simply by effort. Tracking times and logging workouts invite negative comparisons, they said. While times and totals motivate and encourage accountability in beginning runners, these can add stress to runners who are going to run anyway and don't need a constant reminder of how that running differs from the past.

> *If you're going to keep beating yourself up that you're not*
> *getting the times, it is just making training hard and unpleasant.*
> *I just go out how I feel; I go run. It is more free and open.*
> —COLLEEN DE REUCK

Finger on the Pulse

Clearly the mental benefits of training by feel are enormous. And, as it turns out, the physical benefits are too.

Most lifetime runners have a story about getting injured in their 40s as a result of trying to match their training from earlier years in distance, pace, or both. Training by effort addresses these difficulties in one swoop. If you're tuned in to what a tempo run feels like, or a long run, or a workout at 5K effort, your pace will naturally follow as your ability changes. In contrast, if you try to match arbitrary paces, either what you have always done or in order to follow a generalized age-based formula that doesn't account for your unique experience, you'll have to increase your effort when perhaps you shouldn't.

If you listen to your body, running hard when you feel good and backing off when you don't, you'll also automatically add the increased recovery time your body needs as you age without having to modify your schedule and lament that you can't do what you used to. If you throw out the plan entirely and run as far as your body lets you, being careful to listen when it tells you to rest, you'll land on the right level of volume that you need, avoiding either extreme of cutting back too little and getting hurt or cutting back too much and losing fitness.

Some will hear all this and still prefer to follow a schedule. That is perfectly fine, but tuning in to effort is still part of the process. Even with a schedule, you must be willing to adapt to what you are capable of doing and how you are responding. To do that, you need to pay attention to how you feel; you'll need to know yourself.

Walter Bortz, professor of medicine and a masters marathoner, wrote in his book *The Roadmap to 100*, "If there were a first rule of longevity, it would be the command *'Know Thyself,'* handed down to us from the Delphic Oracle some 3000 years ago. Our bodies constantly give us feedback on our internal workings." The ability to run by feel is the result of knowing yourself.

WHAT SHOULD I DO TODAY?

Effort-based training isn't a tool only to employ as you age. Many of the most successful lifetime competitors approached running this way from the beginning. Training by effort frees you from the tyranny of the training schedule and the watch; protects you from overtraining; helps you discover your strengths, your limits, and the type of training that works best for you; and removes much of the stress—at whatever your age.

To learn how to train by effort requires changes in habits and tools. You have to leave your GPS watch behind (or learn to ignore it). If you do look at a watch, discipline yourself to treat it simply as information—this is what pace this effort level feels like today—not as a judgment or a guide to how hard you should run.

Many runners who train by effort find the GPS can be helpful in that it keeps track without you having to. But consider checking it *after* the run to find out what pace that effort level was on this day or on a specific repeat or hill. Looking at it every mile and speeding up or slowing down based on the numbers you see is counterproductive. You must instead tune in to what feels right for the workout and trust yourself.

Admittedly, that trust gets tested as you age and slow down. If a tempo run has always been in, say, the 5:50 to 6:10 range, as it was for me during my 20s and 30s, it's hard to accept when that same level of perceived effort only gets you 6:40 to 7:00 miles. But those who age best find ways to do so, having learned to trust their knowledge of the effort, not the watch. That trust comes from paying attention at every age.

You can also benefit by moving your speed work off the track, away from the too accurate, controlled distance that begs to be constantly measured, quantified, and judged. Rest assured you can get as good or better a workout away from the oval.

In his training book *Little Black Book, Redux*, elite coach Brad Hudson wrote, "A fartlek can be used to accomplish just about anything you can do on the track . . . Sometimes it is just as beneficial to do a hard workout by placing the emphasis on the feel and effort rather than being tied to pace and distance."

Magill, a coach, agrees, writing in *Running Times*: "To avoid the trap of training by pace, we go off-track for our workouts. This eliminates the temptation to check split times during our reps. It also allows us to practice adjusting for race-day variables: weather, terrain, our fatigue level, etc. The ability to adjust for variables is essential to race-day success."

Feel isn't only about the hard days, either. New York City masters runner Alan Ruben, 60, pays attention and adjusts his training based on how *easy* a run feels. He finds he can assess his fitness without having to push. "I test myself by how easily I can run a particular pace, how easy it feels," he said.

To do this, you need to focus and assess yourself on both easy and hard days. Ruben runs the same loop every morning and times how long he takes. After each run, he, like Benoit Samuelson, can compare how hard it felt to run that known time and distance. If you lack such a bench-mark, this is an instance when you do need a watch or GPS—not to see if you're going fast enough but rather to have an empirical time to measure your level of effort against. Learning to assess levels of easy can save you from the need to always push the limits in order to test yourself, and thus, overdo it.

Learning to Cook

To truly train by effort, you also can't be too closely tied to a daily training schedule. If you do follow one, you at least must be willing to alter it regularly, without guilt or reserve. This requires a considerable knowledge of training and your own body, however, which takes time and experimentation. While many lifetime competitors follow an effort-based schedule as masters, few, if any, started that way.

In this regard, the charts and information in training books and articles are important and useful. To use Allen's analogy, you can't bake bread with no experience by simply dumping random ingredients into a bowl. You have to have a good idea of which ingredients, in which proportion, must be added at which time. Only after following recipes enough to thoroughly understand them and how changing variables alter the results can you relax and start playing with the ingredients and proportions.

Similarly, in order to confidently know what feels appropriate on a given day, you have to learn how to taste the mix and in doing so, know which ingredient is lacking. Those who are very good at this can sense what type of workout or drills their bodies need on any given day, what ingredient or spice will perfect the dish of their race-ready fitness.

In his book *Run: The Mind-Body Method of Running by Feel*, Matt Fitzgerald delves into this ability to sense what is right, which he calls intuition, and concurs that this ability is based on experience. Thus, he says, "Beginners must learn and apply the proven, general best practices of training, relying on such authoritative knowledge almost entirely to direct the course of their training until they have gathered enough experience to begin receiving intuitions. The more experienced they become, the more they can rely on intuition."

Focus on the Effect, Not the Record

Most importantly, training by effort requires a change in mindset about how training works. Training by effort recognizes that what is important is the training's effect on the body, not the numbers recorded in a log. It requires relaxing and ignoring the voices that question if you're working hard enough and needle you to accumulate miles and splits to buck up your ego.

> *Training by effort recognizes that what is important is the training's effect on the body, not the numbers recorded in a log.*

If you went out and did the work, and you're healthy and ready to do it again tomorrow, then you're ahead of the game. Believe that you are fit because you feel fit, and because you can run fast when you want and long when you want, not because of your impressive Strava feed or that you've followed a certain training plan to a T.

Avoid comparing your distances and paces with others. Remember, what works for them is only marginally related to what works for you. Everyone's reaction to training is different; everyone's recovery needs are different. Save the comparisons for the racecourse.

Roy Benson, a lifetime competitor and the author of books on heart rate, wrote in a *Running Times* article, "You can correctly run any workout you want, if you run it at the right effort for you. Because effort, not your teammates or training buddies, dictates how fast you should run a hard workout or how slowly you should run an easy workout."

Training successfully by effort also requires that you stop treating every run as a test. Even a race-specific workout is simply a workout designed to stress us so that we rebuild stronger.

Said Magill, "We don't run repetitions to practice running faster. We run repetitions to improve the physiological systems that will allow us to run faster in the future. To accomplish this goal, we train 5K 'effort' rather than 5K 'pace.' As our fitness improves, our pace will improve. But our perceived effort will remain the same, allowing us to become well-versed in the effort level we'll use in the race itself."

How Do You Learn It?

Learning to train by effort is a process, one that improves over time. And it is closely intertwined with the qualities discussed in previous chapters. Running must be *consistent*, a daily habit, part of your identity. The question can't be whether you feel good enough to run today (except on the rare occasions when you are flirting with illness or injury). The assessment of pace, distance, and workout comes only after you're already out the door on your habitual run, warmed up and ready to roll.

You also have to be committed to training at a *variety of paces*, from sprints to tempo runs to easy long runs, progressions, and repeats. If what you feel like doing is going easy every day, you won't get race fit and you'll be more prone to injury.

As we saw, many top competitors still follow a rough schedule even when relying on perceived effort to control the details. Those who don't follow a schedule have developed a desire, born of habit, to feel variety regularly. Thus they will choose to push the hills one day and go long on another, speed up during a run to make it a progression, finishing in a joyful sprint, or cruise at a fast-but-not-hard tempo pace during another run.

Top runners' examples show us that to be a competitor who trains by effort also requires pushing at the limits. The question must be, "What can I get away with?" in terms of doing more miles and pushing the pace, rather than, "How little can I do and still accomplish this goal?" The goal is always to do your best, regardless of where that falls out.

Part of judging your own appropriate effort is to have pushed over the edge at some point, to know your warning signs, and then to have the discipline to come close but not push past the next time.

Ideally, you learned these limits and warning signs as a younger runner and stay clear of the edge as a master, since the consequences are greater for older athletes. "For the senior athlete, not training means that the rate at which aerobic capacity and muscle mass are lost accelerates," warns Friel in *Fast After 50*. "What may have been a half percentage point lost per year now doubles (or worse)."

Every Breath You Take

If you don't know what different training paces feel like, the first step is to start paying attention. One place to focus is your breathing. Coates, experimenting with his own running and with others' as a coach, developed an advanced breathing system in which you breathe in for one more step than you breathe out. Among the many benefits of adopting this method, described in his book *Running on Air*, is learning how to judge

INTERNALIZING THE COACH

When you train by effort, you essentially make yourself the coach, making decisions on workouts and paces. Many runners who do this successfully have the voice of a former coach in their heads guiding those decisions.

Rolf Westphal, a Maine native, has been a runner since grade school and is still running strong at 53. I ran just behind Westphal in cross-country and track in the late '70s and chased him again in 2016 at the Millinocket Half-Marathon, where he won the 50–59 division in a strong 1:29 on a hilly course and a freezing day.

Westphal falls toward the unstructured end of the train-by-feel spectrum. "I just try to get out there and get the miles in," he told me. "I don't schedule my workouts. I'm not going to say, 'I'm going to do a hard 8 miles today.' I just run by feel." He's never downloaded a training schedule or followed one in a book or magazine.

His training, however, isn't random. To this day, he follows the patterns set by his high school coach at Mount Desert Island High School, Howie Richards, who also coached Allen. Richards's pattern was based on Lydiardesque training periods, with summer miles advancing to hills then sharpening with intervals to a peak.

Westphal runs consistently, about 40 miles a week. He still gets in a base of miles, like he did during high school summers. When he has a race approaching, he adds hill workouts and then puts in a bit more speed, just as he did approaching the championships at the end of cross-country season decades ago.

The workouts are more relaxed and effort-based now than they were at Mount Desert Island. "I'm not out there doing half-mile intervals on the track," he said. "I do fartlek stuff, run telephone poles—a couple hard, a couple easy—and I'll do hill workouts."

When he calls himself "old school," he's exactly right. Westphal's training looks a lot like what we learned in school 30, 40, or more years ago. He and many others who now train by feel at one time had a strong coach who gave them the parameters around which they base their training today.

Grimes praises his coach at Humboldt State University, Jim Hunt, for the way in which he educated as well as directed his teams. "Guys who went to Humboldt had a reputation of being able to coach themselves," Grimes said. "Our coach didn't only say, 'Do this,' but he would explain why we were doing this. We learned the purpose of all of our workouts. We learned the process we had to go through to get to a certain point." Now, Grimes runs by feel, but he knows what ingredients he needs in his training because of his apprenticeship under Hunt.

The voice of a coach in your head, interacting with self-monitoring, is a winning combination for many experienced masters. But if you lack such a voice or mentor, all is not lost: Many lifetime competitors who had poor coaches learned the principles by becoming students of the sport, a key we will explore in Chapter 8, and thus became their own coaches.

---

different paces based on what breathing pattern you need to run them. Once you've learned this pattern, it doesn't change.

Coates said that when he developed the breathing plan in 1990, he learned that when running intervals he needed a 3-2 pattern (3 steps breathing in, 2 steps out). "Now, at 60, it is the same effort, 3-2," he said. "The times are different, but I'm working just as hard, I'm getting that same feeling."

Coates uses this perception to guide his training. "I don't even look at the watch anymore," Coates said, whether running intervals or long runs.

Whether or not you follow Coates's specific rhythms isn't as important as learning to feel the different breathing efforts of each training pace. Breathing is strongly correlated with effort across the range of paces. One transition point, near your tempo run pace, is called the ventilatory threshold, the point at which you need to start breathing harder to keep up with oxygen demands. Paying attention to this transition can help you learn what running at that threshold feels like. That threshold is based on your current fitness and, unlike set paces, will go up when you get more fit and down when you age. Learn it once, however, and it will feel the same your whole life.

Effort and Race Time Goals

It's all well and good to train by feel if your goals are flexible and you are simply running whatever you can do on a given day. Many said they race this way now as masters: Rather than setting a goal and training toward it, they train because that is what they do, and when they start to feel fit, they take that strength out for a spin to see what it can do in a race.

However, what if you're aiming for a PR or a Boston qualifier? Don't you then need to train to meet that time, those splits?

The truth is that you can run only as fast as you can run today. Trying to run workouts pegged to a goal time does little good if your body isn't ready to run at that level. You'll push too hard and end up hurt or toasted. On the flip side, sticking to a prescribed pace may limit you if your body would let you go faster at the appropriate effort level.

Asked how she reconciles a time goal with running by feel, Benoit Samuelson said she times her training loops, which she's run for years, so she knows after the run what pace she hit. Based on this information, she knows roughly what race shape she's in. She'll train at the effort level and pace that feels right and then, if she knows she's got a shot based on the times she's running, she'll set the goal, rather than the other way around.

Kastor trains similarly. Her workouts are mostly effort based, with time incentives provided by her coach to motivate her and let her know when she's ready. Rather than monitoring her times constantly during workouts, she says she runs hard and then sees if it is enough.

"Once I could hit these certain times, I knew I could reach my goal," she said.

For her, it's the effort first, then the affirmation. "It is pushing my limits and working hard, and then in the end, looking at what the times were," Kastor said.

HEART RATE AND FEEL

Another way to learn effort is to correlate what you feel with what a heart rate monitor tells you at various paces.

Tracking your heart rate will give you an empirical number to assure you that you're working in roughly the right range. Over time, however, as you get used to the perceived effort of each type of workout, that perceived effort becomes the best measure, one that is more reliable than heart rate. Heart rate lags behind when effort changes, and it can be affected by your emotional state, how much coffee you drank that morning, or other factors unrelated to your running effort. Perceived effort will also endure as a reliable measure throughout the decades of your running life, even as your maximum heart rate changes with age.

To assist in learning perceived effort, Benson created an Effort-Based Training Correlations Chart. The left column tells the reason for running at this pace, and the middle column provides the percentage of your heart rate reserve. Research the Karvonen Formula to calculate your heart rate reserve zone, which takes into account both maximum and resting heart rate. The third column gives a description of what the effort feels like at that pace, and the final column lists common names for these efforts, which you'll find in training plans and conversations with other runners.

EFFORT-BASED TRAINING CORRELATIONS CHART

Reasons for the Workout	At % of Effort (of Max O_2 uptake)	So Perceived Exertion Will Feel Like	Commonly Called
1. Maintain endurance while getting maximum recovery before a race	Slogging at 60–65%	It's too easy; like absolutely no work is being done. It's biomechanically awkward to jog so slowly and difficult to even work up a sweat.	Recovery Run
2. Help muscles recover glycogen stores by burning fat as primary fuel	Jogging at 65–70%	It's worth doing; you can at least work up a sweat. You can carry on a full conversation. It's a fast jog, and you are not tired at the end.	Easy Run
3. Develop local muscle endurance and mental patience	Loping long and easy at 65–75%	It's a fast jog/slow run; it's easy to talk. You're rather weary from such a long time on your feet, and you might want a nap to recover. You thought you would never get to the end of the workout.	Long Run
4. Prepare muscles to make the transition from aerobic to anaerobic running	Striding steadily at 75–80%	It's a faster pace, but easy enough to sustain. You can still talk in short sentences between gasps; it's your half-marathon (novice) to marathon pace (expert).	Rhythm Run/ Steady-State Run
5. Improve anaerobic threshold	Galloping hard at tempo pace at 80–85%	You're running a time trial; you're huffing and puffing too hard to talk. It's uncomfortable but sustainable for 2–4 miles and close to your 15K race pace (novice) to half-marathon pace (expert).	Tempo Run
6. Increase your max O_2 and improve mental toughness	Really running speed work at 90–95%	It's very fast, but not all out. You have enough left to kick the last 100 m. It's pain, torture, and agony.	VO_2Max/ 5K Pace
7. Improve lactic acid tolerance, get very, very tough mentally, and learn to relax as you tie up	Almost sprinting at 95–100%	It's significantly faster than race pace. Your legs are full of lead; you are tying up as you near the finish. You are close to full sprint speed. It's over so quick that it fools your HRM.	Pure Speed Workouts

Used with permission from Roy Benson, adapted from a chart that first appeared in his column in *Running Times*, May 2007.

A key part of this strategy is to not announce your goal until you know you are in range. That's why Benoit Samuelson said she had not yet formally announced her dream of running sub-3:00 at 60. "It is a goal I have, and it is going to be a challenge for me," she said. The effort-based training will have to tell her it's doable before she'll tell the world.

When the world's best runners say this, it makes perfect sense: How can you set a goal that is beyond your fitness to achieve? You can have a long-term goal that stands out there, at the end of the season or even several years away, but progress toward it will be incremental as your body and racing ability improve.

Many of us, however, start with the goal and try to run workouts that will make it possible. And many of us get hurt trying to do that training, or, on race day, we go out too hard and blow up. Turning it around and learning to judge effort, in training and racing, will lead to both success and longevity.

KEY 3
TRAINING BY FEEL

- Ignore the clock: Learn to judge a workout by its perceived effort, not the time on your watch.
- Get flexible: Let your body, not a predetermined plan, dictate your pace and distance.
- Learn to cook: Combine proven training ingredients to best suit your strengths and preferences, tasting the results daily and adjusting as necessary.
- Feel the wind: Enjoy being able to feel fast and fit at any age, untethered to times.

THE KEYS PART TWO

PSYCHOLOGICAL PRINCIPLES

5

HUMILITY AND HUNGER
THE PROMISE OF HUMBLE BEGINNINGS

> If you really want to enjoy life, you must work quietly
> and humbly to realize your delusions of grandeur.
>
> —MARK HELPRIN, *A SOLDIER OF THE GREAT WAR*

I've now coached high school kids long enough to see a generation of them grow up. One thing I've learned is that those who continue running past college and into their adult lives often aren't the ones you expect to.

The state champions, the school record setters, the ones with the most medals and trophies at their graduation receptions often no longer run. The ones who are still running at age 25 or 30 and beyond tend to have been number four or five on the team, or even runners who never placed. The girl who didn't run track but trained herself and ran a half-marathon in high school is more likely to be on a starting line a decade later than the one who was identified in junior high as a natural and set meet records in seventh grade.

Knowing this, I should not have been surprised by what I heard from lifetime competitors about their own humble beginnings and their perspectives on their abilities. But I was. It's hard not to be dazzled by what they have accomplished in running, how high they have climbed and how fast they still are. But nearly without exception, these runners told me that they were never that good, or if good, not by any means great.

ALMOST GOOD

Robinson started running as a schoolboy in England in the 1950s. By 1966, running with a club as a PhD student in England, he qualified for the national team at the World Cross Country Championships. After moving to New Zealand and excelling on the road and grass there, Robinson competed as part of his new country's national cross-country team at age 38.

Entering the masters ranks, he shone even brighter, winning the World Masters 10K Road Championships and setting masters records at the Vancouver, Boston, and New York City Marathons.

Despite all of his success, one of the first things Robinson told me when we sat down to talk at 2016's Boston Marathon was that he was never very good.

"I was almost good," he said.

When he started in school, Robinson was enthusiastic, but today says he had limited talent and strength. "I was never the best," he said. Nonetheless, he was persistent. "I eventually won the school cross-country championship, but that was my last year."

Robinson was one of the first interviewed for this book, and I figured he was just unusually humble. By the 50th interview, however, I had heard this sentiment so many times that I knew there was something significant about it.

Eventually, I began to wait for it. After telling about the motivation that got them into running, often tied to their utter failure at other sports, lifetime competitors would say some variation of "I wasn't very good." Here are few of them:

"I came pretty close to dead last all the time. It seemed everybody was really, really good, except me." —PHIL PILLIN

"I'm not a talented person." —KATHRINE SWITZER

"My freshman year, I finished second to last in state cross-country. I was glad to beat somebody." —JOHN MIRTH

"I was good locally, not great. I kept improving, but I wasn't by any means one of the fastest." —LEONARD SPERANDEO

"It's not like I was a great success. I never went to the state meet. Never set the world on fire. I couldn't really run fast." —CRAIG CHRISTIANS

"I wasn't a superstar." —KELLY KRUELL

"I wasn't really good until I was out of college." —BENJI DURDEN

"I was very much second tier, in their shadow." —DAVE GRIFFIN

While each of these runners went on to become very good indeed, they never thought of themselves that way. Even those with early success had a keen awareness of where they fit in the running world, how much better others were. Their vision was always aimed forward at what they could become, not what they had accomplished.

Burfoot, the winner of the 1968 Boston Marathon, admitted he started out quite good, winning the state 2 mile a year after he got into the sport. Nevertheless, he revealed his upward-focused mindset when talking about his ability. "When I'm asked how good I was, I say I was good enough to get to the level where I could get on the track with Gerry Lindgren and Jim Ryun and learn that I wasn't good enough," Burfoot said. "There were others a whole lot better than me."

THE DANGER OF WINNING

When I considered the athletes I have coached and those I interviewed for this book who have quit the sport, a humble worldview among lifetime competitors is a pattern that begins to make a lot of sense. One of the greatest dangers to longevity in the sport, it seems, is early success and recognition. That danger comes in two forms.

One danger of being good is that you win and get awards. Those awards feel good, and you want more of them. On the one hand, this can motivate you to train and get better, which is a good thing. "Being successful is an adrenaline ego buzz, and it breeds more striving for success," Burfoot said.

Like Burfoot, Dunham said, "I was pretty successful, and that's what kept me at it. Nothing like doing well to motivate you to do more."

As they continued in the sport, Burfoot and Dunham learned to love the running as much as the winning. Some, however, get attached to those awards and accolades. Nearly every lifetime runner told me stories about talented fellow runners who no longer run because they can't win anymore.

Durden cited several elites he used to run with who quit when they found they could no longer be contenders. Running, for them, never was that much fun, they told him.

For these runners, the results were the motivation and running was simply the means to an end. When this happens, the activity loses its intrinsic pleasure—the joy of doing it for its own sake—and thus serves no purpose when those rewards decline or end.

The danger of rewards is the subject of Daniel H. Pink's book *Drive: The Surprising Truth About What Motivates Us*. Pink describes how replacing natural motivation with external rewards and punishments can produce unintended results. External rewards can incite people to cheat, they only work if the rewards keep increasing, and they can limit people from doing their best, as you only need to do enough to get the reward. One of those most insidious consequences is that things we enjoy lose their appeal.

"Rewards can perform a weird sort of behavioral alchemy," Pink wrote. "They can transform an interesting task into a drudge. They can turn play into work."

Winning is powerful. It can inspire you. But it is also addictive and can rob you of other meaningful goals.

"If winning is your sole purpose, at some point, running is going to get frustrating," Kastor told me. You can't always win, and as you age, you no longer will be able to win.

It's not that winning never mattered to lifetime competitors or that they haven't set goals to win races. In fact, they worked hard in order to win some, and they cherish those victories. But, significantly, they didn't win from the start; they had to improve and work for it, and it was along that humbling journey where they seemed to have learned the value of running apart from the rewards.

THE DANGER OF TALENT

A second danger of early success is that runners begin to believe they are talented. Parents and coaches laud their ability and tell them they have a gift. They begin to think of success as a result of who they are rather than a result of the work they have done.

The difference between an emphasis on talent versus valuing effort is the theme of psychologist Carol Dweck's book *Mindset: The New Psychology of Success*. Dweck describes two different views of the world:

the *fixed mindset*, which believes abilities are natural and carved in stone, or the *growth mindset*, which sees qualities as things you can cultivate and improve. These different views of the world affect pretty much everything, including running and racing.

For runners with a fixed mindset, the purpose of running and racing becomes to prove their talent. When they race, they must win, ideally with less effort than others. "If you have to work at something, you must not be very good at it," Dweck quotes those with a fixed mindset.

In her book *Grit: The Power of Passion and Perseverance*, Angela Duckworth describes her concerns over those who have early success. "I worry about people who cruise through life, friction-free, for a long, long time before encountering their first real failure," she wrote. "They have so little practice falling and getting up again. They have so many reasons to stick with a fixed mindset."

If you have been good in a small pond and are constantly reinforced for that success, you may seem confident, you may walk with a swagger, but you may actually be vulnerable. "I see a lot of invisibly vulnerable high achievers stumble in young adulthood and struggle to get up again," Duckworth wrote. "I call them the 'fragile perfects.'"

If you're a younger athlete, you have to deal with a tendency to want to preserve your status as a prodigy and gifted athlete. It's far less satisfying to always be proving yourself. The default expected result is to win; losing is a failure. You can never exceed expectations, others' or your own.

The temptation can easily become to play it safe and make sure you always look good, or have a good excuse. You can't risk new challenges that might show that you aren't as special as you've been led to believe.

"A fixed mindset about ability leads to pessimistic explanations of adversity, and that, in turn, leads to both giving up on challenges and avoiding them in the first place," Duckworth wrote. "In contrast, a growth mindset leads to optimistic ways of explaining adversity, and that, in turn, leads to perseverance and seeking out new challenges that will ultimately make you even stronger."

Kastor admits to having a fixed mindset early in her career. "I just thought I had talent, and I didn't understand how to nurture that talent," she said. "I thought when I won races, it was because I was talented, and if I lost races, I wasn't talented enough." After college, frustrated with the sport, she was about to quit, but a conversation with coach Joe Vigil convinced her otherwise.

"Coach Vigil made me believe that I could be better if I applied myself," Kastor said. "In that moment, pursuing running no longer seemed scary. I had a belief that I had it in me to be better." Vigil instilled a growth mindset that has carried her even beyond her pro years.

"The surprising aspect this late in my career has been that progress never stops," Kastor said. "Although my 2:19 may be the fastest I ever run, I really feel that running has taught me to push my limits and my boundaries, and learn how to grow spiritually and mentally. It is my avenue for growth; I'll never retire from it."

In contrast, fixed mindset people don't talk about growth or pushing back boundaries. They hate failures and difficulties; setbacks cause them to question their gifts and their identity. Repeated failure is reason to quit, as it shows that you don't have, or no longer have, the required talent to be somebody. Success is unambiguous: You're a winner or a loser.

Those with a growth mindset, however, relish difficulties as a chance to get better. "The growth mindset allows people to value what they're doing *regardless of the outcome*," Dweck wrote. "[It] allows people to love what they are doing—and to continue to love it in the face of difficulties."

Lifetime competitors tend to have a growth mindset. Instead of seeing early mediocre performances as an indicator that they lacked talent, they were inspired to improve. Instead of quitting when they didn't reach their dreams, they became, and remained, hungry.

Those with a growth mindset
relish difficulties as a chance to get better.

REACH SHOULD EXCEED YOUR GRASP

As lifetime competitors repeatedly remarked on how ungifted they were, it became clear to me that this lack of natural ability, whether real or perceived, helped them to avoid these common pitfalls. What's more, I began to hear how that humble perception of their skill made them hungry and how that hunger led to a love of improvement and an emphasis on mastery that has helped them continue to thrive through the decades.

Instead of starting good and trying to maintain and prove that innate skill, they learned a more important lesson: that they could get better. After telling me about not being very good, competitors would inevitably talk about how they improved. They'd tell how they got better in college or when they got out on their own and started training for road races.

Pillin didn't see much external success until he was an adult runner. He barely made varsity by the end of high school and never was on the traveling team in college, yet he kept training twice a day for years and eventually ran a 2:32 marathon.

All the lifetime competitors reveal a pattern of progression. And they learned to appreciate this process of getting better as much as achieving success. This perspective becomes even more essential when the external indicators of success change.

Even Kastor, despite all of her empirical success, learned to value improvement more than the glory, which is why she can continue to care and enjoy training and competing.

"Progressing, even in the smallest way, is so rewarding," Kastor said. "That has really been the reward of running. It hasn't really been the medals or accolades or the records. It has been those moments of clearly seeing you've created a stronger version of yourself."

Those proofs of progress occur most clearly within races, but the training, the daily running, provides similar rewards as well. It is a cycle of goals, progress, and belief.

"Running is rewarding in itself, because even though you have that end goal, the progress comes every day when you get out there and put in the work," Kastor said. "Each and every day you're getting out there you're actually chipping away at that goal and reinforcing a belief that it is possible."

This belief is the essence of the growth mindset. Robinson called it the runner's mindset. "If you do the work, you will get better," he said. And it is along this ever-present journey toward improvement that the satisfaction lies.

"There was always that wanting," he said. "Feeling I'd like to be better but really having to work for it. It never came easy." Quoting poet Robert Browning, Robinson adds: "A man's reach should exceed his grasp, or what is heaven for?"

Lang has felt a similar pull, the allure of dreams just out of his grasp. "I always was dreaming," Lang said. "Always thought I could get the school record. Could get to state. Never did. I thought maybe I could make the Olympic Trials. That was a goal. Never got there."

Rather than disappointing him, however, those unrealized dreams kept him engaged in the sport. "I never felt like I got to my potential, so I just continued to run," he said. "I found I could keep doing this and see if I can get better. And I did."

Mirth attributes his longevity and continued incentive, at least in part, to never making a state track meet. His younger brother was a state champion in the 2 mile, so Mirth had that example that it was possible. (Interestingly, Mirth says his brother no longer competes.)

"My being on the edge of success, not quite achieving the state meet or All-American honors, left me hungry for proving myself," Mirth said. That hunger, he said, hasn't abated for 40 years.

Even those at the very top of running success revealed that they kept motivated beyond the wins because they never reached the edge of their dreams, never ran the perfect race.

"I loved how once I'd accomplish something, another goal would energize and excite me," Kastor said. "I always feel like there could have been more. I think that is why so many of us continue to get out there."

Robinson said that this feeling of unrealized potential not only motivated him to improve, it is a big reason he continued as an adult. And it paid off. One of the benefits of keeping going is that you may actually get better compared to your peers, both because people age differently and because others fall away.

"There was always, 'If I keep up at this a bit longer, I could get a bit better,'" Robinson said. "I did, relatively, I kept improving. No way I could win a world championship at 35, but I could when I was 40 and 50."

Lang is still aware that he never was as good as he dreamed he'd be, nor as good as those he ran with in high school and college, but he's having the last laugh. "People ask me, people I ran with, can I beat them now?" he says. And he can. "I outlasted them all."

MASTERY AS MOTIVATOR

Whether or not they ever got fast enough to beat others, lifetime competitors said they found continual motivation in chasing mastery. Many runners are obsessed by the challenge of getting better, of becoming the best possible runner they can be given their talents and current conditions.

No one has described the feeling and process of mastery better than Mihaly Csikszentmihalyi in *Flow: The Psychology of Optimal Experience*. While most associate flow with peak out-of-body experiences, the theory explains why doing something well is so satisfying on any day.

The key, Csikszentmihalyi explains, is to find an activity for which the challenge exactly meets your skill, so you have to focus all of your mental and physical energy on it. Too low a challenge results in boredom, too high and you get overwhelmed and withdraw. Low challenge and low skill is comfortable but not very satisfying. The higher the challenge and the skill, the more you can lose yourself in the task and the more satisfying it is.

"The best moments," Csikszentmihalyi wrote, "usually occur when a person's body or mind is stretched to its limits in a voluntary effort to accomplish something difficult and worthwhile."

Flow, a feeling of being powerful and in control, occurs when we face a challenge and think, *This is really hard—but I can do it. I've got this.* This feeling of mastery is something lifetime runners crave.

Grimes described it in terms of how he feels on the run. "When I am in shape, I go for a run and it is not work," he said. "Even if I run really hard, I don't perceive it as work. You just feel good. That's the thing about being in shape—even the effort feels good."

He finds that this is what motivates him, being fit enough to maintain this feeling. That feeling, untethered from absolute, arbitrary marks, is what it is all about for him.

Kastor relishes the focus needed to match a difficult challenge. "When I get to that crux of a workout or crux of a race, it takes a lot of mental effort to get through that—that's what thrills me," she said. And she noted how this thrill is not linked to the clock. "We can progress in other ways that aren't on the watch. I think that is why I still love doing this."

MY BEST TODAY

A race provides one of the best contexts to experience mastery, which is a big reason why lifetime competitors keep competing. "I find great lessons when I push my limits. I learn I can endure more than I ever thought possible," Kastor said.

It's notable that while mastery is about doing well, it's not tied to perfection. You never achieve perfection, but you can achieve mastery on a given day. Mastery is about doing your best given the challenges of that day. Those challenges include time and distance, as always, but also the terrain, the weather, your work schedule, the competition, and even the iffy restaurant food you may have had the night before.

Those conditions also include age. Dealing with being 52 is no different from dealing with a hot, hilly course. Both will result in slower times than a perfect day on a flat course when you're in the best shape of your life. In the end, the question you answer for yourself is whether you mastered the challenge.

"That is why I keep doing it, this whole test of what it takes to do your best, whatever your best is," Kevin Paulk told me. Paulk races in masters track meets, with the 800 m his forte. At age 43, he was able to run 1:58. Now, in his 50s, a good time is closer to 2:15.

Slowing times aren't significant to him, however the effort and mastery are. "If 2:15 today is the best I could do, then that is victory," Paulk says. "If I know I ran as hard as I possibly could and I prepared to do that really well, that is absolute victory."

Kastor's experience at the 2015 Chicago Marathon brought this perspective into sharp relief. "On the starting line, I had a million reasons why I couldn't fulfill my goal of breaking the masters record," she said. She'd had the flu a week earlier, forest fires near her home in California had restricted her training and inflamed her allergies, and she had been traveling a lot for work.

Rather than giving up, however, she moved past the excuses and gave herself pep talks as she experienced the difficulties in the race. "When it got really hard, at 21 miles, at first I was like, *This is going to be a death march,*" she said. "Then I thought, *Wait a second. This is why I still run. This is the moment when I have the opportunity to grow, as an athlete and as a person.*"

She focused on meeting the challenges and mastering the day. To do so, she had to redefine the challenge into something she could believe her skills were up to meeting. "I finally got to a place where I was still on pace, taking one mile at a time, and celebrating each one," she said. "I made it to the finish line and made my goal."

Never mind that her 2:27:47 was six minutes slower than the 2:21:25 she ran to win Chicago in 2005. She considers the 2015 race one of her greatest accomplishments, a race where she ran as close to her best as she ever had before, even if the time was slower.

"A lot of times our great races come on that flawless day when it feels so good, you feel like you could run forever," Kastor said. "This day, I was able to get to the same place on a day that was very subpar, with a subpar buildup, because of that mental strength."

WHY IT MATTERS

Humility and hunger aren't optional for those who want to continue to pursue excellence through the years. The alternatives, hubris and complacency, won't get us out the door and, in fact, encourage quitting to avoid the appearance of failure. Conventional wisdom says that we need to find what we're good at, what comes easy for us, and then reap the low-hanging fruits of success that our natural talent produces. Those who persist, however, are often the ones who weren't given all the gifts but developed skill and learned to appreciate growth and mastery.

The fact that many lifetime competitors started out as poor or average runners, at least in their minds, is certainly encouraging. It indicates you don't necessarily need natural talent to experience mastery or flow, and you don't need to be at a certain level to get hooked by the satisfaction of getting better. In fact, you might even be at an advantage, as you can avoid the pitfalls that accompany the rewards and accolades of success.

Coach Chris Bennett built the Nike+ Run Club program around this idea that personal progress is the goal. He believes that everyone can love running if they are challenged and given a chance to be better. He starts with wherever a runner is, whether that be an inexperienced, unathletic teenager new to running, an out-of-shape mid-lifer who shows up at a club workout one night, or someone with an abundance of natural talent.

"Who you are today, that's the basis of everything," Bennett said, explaining his philosophy when I visited him on the Nike campus in 2016. "If you tell me you suck, I want you to suck less. If you tell me you're awesome, I want you to be more awesome by the end of the workout." He'll treat you the same and give you the same goal. Wherever you start that day, he says, the goal of the workout for one and all is "just to be a little bit better."

Those who persist are often the ones who weren't given all the gifts but developed skill and learned to appreciate growth and mastery.

Bennett described the feeling of mastery he sees in the eyes of runners every week. "You can see it dancing in their eyes," he said. "When they realize, *I beat it. I'm tougher than this workout. It's a tough workout, but I'm tougher.*"

When they realize that running is about this feeling and that this feeling just keeps getting better the better they get, they are on their way to being lifetime competitors. It really has nothing to do with talent at all.

Kastor echoed this idea when she was asked whether running and racing would still motivate her if she couldn't set records. "Absolutely. That's the common denominator in all runners, whether you're trying to break the American record or trying to push your limits and finish your first half-marathon," she said. "We're all out there giving the best we can. The times may look different across the board, but the exertion is the same."

WHAT SHOULD I DO TODAY?

Building humility and hunger is straightforward if you start where many of the lifetime competitors started. You need only to stick with it and, quoting novelist Mark Helprin, "work quietly and humbly to realize your delusions of grandeur."

Lifetime competitors stay humble and hungry by setting challenging and appropriate goals (more on that in Chapter 6) and working to achieve them. The thrill of improvement and the satisfaction of mastery hook them so that they end up unable to imagine life without running.

Mastery isn't about everything going perfectly but rather about rising to the challenges you face. Those challenges range from weather to terrain to career constraints to age. We may wonder what we could do on the perfect day: 45 degrees, no wind, flat course, following six months of solid, focused training. But that day never comes, and even if it did, we would still have the imperfection of our physiology and upbringing. Our best is relative, at any age.

"Perfection belongs to an imaginary world," wrote Thomas Moore in *Care of the Soul.* Every race, at any age, has a footnote listing the specific conditions of the course, the day, and all the details of your life in the weeks, months, even years before it. What you hear from lifetime competitors is an acceptance that today, with all its imperfections, may be as good as it gets. And it is enough.

Get In over Your Head

One thing is clear from lifetime competitors' stories, and that is to always look up rather than down. Focus on runners who are better, and learn the honest humility of comparing your achievements to theirs. No matter who you are, you can find someone better. Put yourself in situations where you aren't the best. Learn to appreciate working hard and getting better, even when it doesn't garner an award. Don't settle for being the fastest runner on your team or in your town. Work humbly and hungrily toward goals just out of reach.

In order to work against a fixed mindset that sees abilities as innate, author Dweck recommends, among other strategies, that you avoid drawing judgments about yourself based on circumstances. If you win a race, it means you ran fast, not that you are fast. A slow race doesn't mean you are slow.

Dweck wrote, regarding successful growth-minded athletes: "None of them thought they were special people, born with the right to win." They put in the work and focused on giving their best efforts rather than on the pecking order or where they "should" be.

Honestly seeing yourself on a regional, national, or global scale can help dissuade any illusions of being special. But remember, this doesn't have to be discouraging. Knowing how much better others are can inspire you to grow. And learning to do your best when you aren't the best prepares you for a time when you can't match the success you have now. Accepting that your success now is relative prepares you for scaling your expectations as you age.

Adopting a growth mindset often isn't easy or welcomed. Dweck acknowledges the difficulty in changing a fixed mindset. "Fixed traits may come to be the person's sense of who they are, and validating these traits may come to be the main source of their self-esteem," she wrote.

It's a tricky thing to reshape an identity, but it can be done. Kastor made the transition after college, going from believing her ability was based on a fixed talent to wanting to work and improve. "It wasn't until post-college that I knew to express my talent better by training really hard and being positive," she said.

Meeting this challenge becomes critical as you age, when you've run your last PR, particularly if you've held on to and reinforced your "fast" identity until then.

De Reuck touched on the process of changing her view of herself when she could no longer compete as a pro. "Initially, switching from being able to win races and get personal best times to going to participate did take a while, I must admit," she said. "You have to switch over your mind to accepting that, because that's life: You get older, you get slower. But it did take a little time to accept it."

De Reuck found that the switch, however, was not painful but a relief. "Once you do that, it's free, it's fun," she said. "You can just go and do things; you're not pressured. The only pressure is what you put on yourself."

Playing with the Equation

Long before the theories of flow or of fixed mindsets, the philosopher William James created an equation that helps explain them. James expressed self-esteem as a fraction.

"Our self-feeling in this world depends entirely on what we back ourselves to be and do," James wrote in *Psychology: The Briefer Course*. "It is determined by the ratio of our actualities to our supposed potentialities." Thus, James wrote: Self-esteem = success / pretensions.

Our pretensions are the sum of our goals and expectations. Looking at the equation, it follows that you can increase your self-esteem either by increasing your success or by decreasing your pretensions.

"To give up pretensions is as blessed a relief as to get them gratified," James wrote. "And where disappointment is incessant and the struggle unending, this is what men will always do."

If, as we age into our 40s, 50s, and beyond, we hold on to expectations that we can accomplish everything we've always done as runners, our disappointment will be incessant and the struggle frustrating and unending. The solution is to change the denominator of the equation: the goals and expectations. And that can be freeing, as De Reuck found.

The idea of lowering expectations can feel like defeat. After all, it's hard to get excited about getting slower. But rather than a passive acceptance of declining abilities or resistance to the challenges of new realities, I found among lifetime competitors myriad inspiring, creative ways to set new goals and change the parameters so that these runners remain as hungry as ever. This adaptability, in terms of goals and training patterns, is the topic of the next two chapters.

KEY 4
HUMILITY AND HUNGER

- Compare up: Be aware of others who are better than you and the potential for progress.
- Reframe adversity: Accept failure as a motivator to work harder and difficulties as opportunities to overcome more challenges.
- Embrace the process: Recognize that running is not a test of talent but a process of growth.
- Personalize success: Learn to appreciate running your best even when you aren't the best.

6

ADAPTABILITY, PART 1
SETTING GOALS

Enjoyment appears at the boundary between
boredom and anxiety, when the challenges are just balanced
with the person's capacity to act.

—MIHALY CSIKSZENTMIHALYI, *FLOW*

As she approached 50, Benoit Samuelson faced a decision. Up until then, the queen of the American marathon was still competing in the lead pack. While she wasn't winning large races anymore, she remained a fierce contender.

"In my mid-40s, I was racing, trying to run as fast as I can. I didn't look at myself as a master runner," she told me.

At 48, she qualified for her seventh Olympic Trials by running a 2:46:27 at the 2006 Twin Cities Marathon, placing 11th overall. Her times, however, were far slower than they had been, and while she never considered quitting running, she was thinking seriously about no longer competing.

"I got slower," she said. "But I'm passionate about the sport. It's part of who I am." She knew she still wanted to compete, but she determined that the nature of her goals had to change. She couldn't win outright, she couldn't set new PRs, and age-group victories didn't excite her.

So she started tying goal times to what she calls "stories."

"When the trials were announced for Boston, I set a goal of running sub-2:50 at 50, where I started my career," she said.

In interviews leading up to the trials, she hinted this would be her swan song. "I think it is pretty cool that I will most likely end my competitive marathoning career where I started my competitive marathoning career almost 30 years earlier."

At the time, however, Benoit Samuelson was also dealing with an injury and debated even starting, as she'd never dropped out of a race before and certainly didn't want to do so at the trials. Despite this uncertainty, she did start and went on to finish under her goal time, running a 2:49:08.

"I accomplished the goal and walked away with Deena and Magdalena [Lewy-Boulet] and Blake Russell," she said. "They waited for me at the finish line, which was really sweet. I thought, *What a way to go out.*"

But then a funny thing happened: She didn't go out. Stories continued to compel her.

The next year she got a call from Mary Wittenberg.

Wittenburg, president of the New York Road Runners, said, "How would you like to come to New York to celebrate the 25th anniversary of your Olympic win and the 40th anniversary of the New York City Marathon?"

Benoit Samuelson thought, *Well, that tells a story.* And off she went to New York.

The next year, Carey Pinkowski, executive race director for the Chicago Marathon, called. "It was the 25th anniversary of my fastest time in Chicago and the date was 10/10/10—and that told a story," Benoit Samuelson said.

Then it was the Athens Marathon, celebrating the 2,500th anniversary of the Battle of Marathon. "*As a marathoner, I really ought to go,*" she recalled thinking.

And so she has run through her 50s, chasing one compelling story after another. In 2013, she ran the Boston Marathon on the 30th anniversary of her fastest time, with a goal of running within 30 minutes of that time. She achieved the goal, and then "all hell broke loose with the bombs, so I had to come back the next year."

The next year was the 30th anniversary of her Olympic victory and the first time her two children ran in a marathon with her. They set a goal of all finishing within 30 minutes of each other.

"It's the stories that motivate me to keep going and keep it fresh," she said. "And then in so doing, I'm told I often motivate others, which is a bonus. I'm doing it to tell my story—if I can pull others along with me, that's pretty cool."

The next story, she said, was to run a marathon in her home state of Maine, which she had never done. She planned to do it the weekend after her 60th birthday alongside Michael Westphal, a high school friend now running marathons with Parkinson's disease, who would also be celebrating his 60th birthday.

And after that? "I'd love to run under 3:00 at 60," she said.

It's an arbitrary number, three hours. But it's a story that compels her, and it is appropriate for her fitness level today. She's not sure she can run sub-3:00—it will take work. The challenge is enough to keep her doing long runs when she finds herself on a nice day with clear roads, racing cars to the next stop sign when she's feeling frisky, and going to yin yoga classes once a week.

While it is challenging, it is also a goal within reach. Benoit Samuelson is not trying to win Chicago or match the PR of 2:21 that she ran there in 1985. She knows that if she can get in the miles and stay healthy, and then focus and race tough, just as she has all her life, she has a good chance of making it. It's the same challenge she's faced for 45 years—the numbers are irrelevant.

Benoit Samuelson said people often question her, asking, "You were giving it up. What's going on?"

She tells them, "I said I was going to give up competitive marathoning. I never said what constitutes competitive."

Runners who can adapt their view of what it means to be competitive and what constitutes success will never run out of challenges and satisfaction.

Benoit Samuelson's recognition that she gets to define what constitutes *competitive* lies at the heart of the strategy many runners use to stay hungry for a lifetime. Runners who can adapt their view of what it means to be competitive and what constitutes success will never run out of challenges and satisfaction.

SCALING THE CHALLENGE

Thriving through decades of running requires adapting. Adapting isn't just important for your athletic survival. Psychologists consider "adaptive competence," the ability to effectively respond to changing conditions, central to flourishing through the years.

In *Successful Aging*, German psychologists Paul and Margaret Baltes reflected on the specific adaptive challenges of getting old. "At first glance, aging and success seem to represent a contradiction," they wrote. "Aging conjures a picture of loss, decline, and approaching death, whereas success connotes gains, winning the game, and a positive balance."

That certainly agrees with most people's view of athletics. Aging and success in sport are contradictory; you get old, you get slow, you get left behind.

Contrary to expectations, however, research has pointed out that many people do age successfully. Research bears out that you can be old and happy, and old and engaged. How? The central task, the Balteses wrote, is "acquiring successful strategies involving changes in aspirations and the scope of goals." In other words, you can stay happy and engaged if you adapt what you aim for and redefine what constitutes being competitive.

Chapter 5 introduced the importance of balancing goals and success. Self-esteem, happiness, and the facilitation of flow all depend on keeping the challenge equal to your skills. To continue to care and strive for excellence—at any age—requires defining the parameters of success. Only one person can be the Olympic marathon champion or the world record holder. Only a few can make state in high school. Successful athletes learn to draw motivation and satisfaction from smaller but still very meaningful goals.

As we age, the added challenge is making peace with the fact that while goals in youth tend to expand, goals as we age will contract; that is, they contract if we hold to a limited view of goals—one confined to absolute numbers.

The key is finding a new goal or a context that means something to you and excites you. That goal will probably be different than it was when you were 20. "Forms and vehicles of 'success' in old age may be different from those in earlier phases of life," the Balteses wrote. More poetically, Somerset Maugham wrote, "Old age has its pleasures, which, though different, are not less than the pleasures of youth."

PICK ON SOMEONE YOUR OWN AGE

Competing within an age group is one simple way to scale your running goals over the years.

Sitting in the kitchen of her house on the coast of Maine, Emery leaned in to me and whispered, "I'm 70 now—look out!" She sat back and laughed. "I couldn't wait to be 70."

At 70, Emery sees a whole new world opening up. She's started looking at bigger races like Beach to Beacon and out-of-state races in Massachusetts. "It opens up this whole thing. I go look at race results— nobody in the 70s. If there are, it's really, really slow."

A pioneer in the sport, Emery won races for many years because she was, at first, the only woman, and then, as others joined the ranks, she was able to take advantage of her head start on serious training.

But when she lost to Benoit in 1976, Emery was disappointed and even considered quitting the sport. "She beat me. I was going to give up," she said. "Like Abrahams in *Chariots of Fire.*"

Her mother, who had initially been resistant to Emery's running, encouraged her to continue. "She's not going to be at every race," her mother told her. "Just do your best."

In addition to learning to deal with having a rival who was consistently better than she was, Emery had to change her view of success from winning outright to competing with those her age. That's not an insignificant adaptation: Many runners told me that they didn't care about age groups for a long time, even after becoming masters. For them, a race is about competing with whoever shows up. The winner crosses the line first; any other distinction is contrived.

Embracing age groups, however, has allowed Emery to keep winning, or at least have the possibility, which has in turn kept her hungry. While she says she'd run even if she couldn't race, she's highly motivated and energized by racing—she ran 43 races last year, at age 69, sometimes two in one weekend.

The age cutoffs are arbitrary, but they give runners like Emery new life every five years. Having achieved a new age group at age 70, she's as excited as a high school freshman entering a new and challenging venue of competition.

Pillin described the feeling of approaching a new level. Last year, he said, he reveled in being 54. Why? Because he thought, *Next year I'll be 55! I'll be in the 55 to 59 age group.* "Can't beat the 50-year-olds anymore, so let's take a shot at the 59-year-olds," he said, laughing.

"Every five years, everything changes," Rodgers said. "Hitting a new age group—it's a fresh new world. We all have a wonderful opportunity again. It is pretty exciting."

> *Every five years, everything changes. Hitting a new age group–*
> *it's a fresh new world. We all have a wonderful opportunity again.*
> –BILL RODGERS

Emery gloated in having turned the page to a new age group. "Now I'm 70," she said. "This is great. Lose to Jeanne Butterfield—not anymore! I love it."

Jeanne Butterfield? "She's my nemesis," Emery said. "But she's four years younger than me. So ha! It's going to be great."

SEARCHING FOR RIVALS

Emery may find, however, that entering a new age group and leaving Jeanne Butterfield behind will leave her with inadequate challenges. More than one lifetime competitor noted that at least in their local region, they didn't have sufficient competition to motivate them. After all, winning won't inspire if you don't have to work for it.

Ringlein, who once ran 34 minutes for the 10K and a 2:47 marathon, just turned 60 and finds herself in age-group limbo. "Not that I was that great, but when you've been as good as I was, if you win the 60-year-olds, it's not that big of a deal," she said. She misses the satisfaction of racing hard for a win.

In the past, she solved that problem by focusing on beating all the masters, in other words, everyone over 40, even when she herself was over 50. Today, on the cusp of 60, she finds she can't do that anymore. "So maybe I have to be happy running with 60-year-olds," she said. She's still figuring out what cutoff, what grouping of competitors, will continue to motivate her to improve but be doable.

Others less gifted may have to scale the other way to find a suitable goal. When I've run in national masters cross-country races, I've finished close to the back, at times even last in my age division. But given the stellar field, I take no shame and indeed find considerable motivation in seeing how many I can beat in the masters field, even if they are 5 to 10 years my senior.

Adapting your goal to a level that keeps you hungry while allowing you occasions to be sated is rarely as easy as accepting age groups. Some find the goal takes the form of a closely matched rival, regardless of age.

Robinson talked about how he feels when his friend and sometimes training partner shows up for a race. "Oh good, Harry's coming!" he'll say. "We'll beat the shit out of each other." He marveled at how it still matters to him. "I'm 76 years old. It is a perpetual childlikeness," he admitted with a laugh.

Ideally, you beat your rival on some days, and on other days, he or she beats you, depending on current training, how well you race, and who wants it more that day. While you can sometimes find head-to-head age competition within a race, having an ongoing rivalry can motivate your training and enliven your racing.

THE WORLD REDUCED TO A SMALL OVAL

Some masters find tremendous motivation and satisfaction on the track, where age groups are separated into different heats so the field that you are racing is clearly defined (and inevitably well prepared).

Paulk waxed eloquent about the beauty of masters track competition. "For me the drive is competing against other human beings," he said. "It's not the clock; it is not how fast did you run. It is how did the race go, racing guys from this line to that line in a footrace."

When the scope is defined by the group on the track, the challenge and experience are timeless. "For me, it is the joy of being able to compete as if I were Matt Centrowitz [1500m gold medalist at the 2016 Olympics]," Paulk said. "Because we're all doing the same thing. We're just not moving as fast! It is quite enjoyable and difficult."

Paulk says masters racing is even better than open competition because of the respect and camaraderie. "The challenge of pushing yourself to the limit and the joy of toeing the line with people our age is one of the most respectful things I've ever experienced in a competitive environment," he said. "We share the same beneficial joy that nothing comes easy. We embrace each other before the gun goes off and after, and we try to kill each other on the track."

TEAMMATES IN THE MUD

Others have found cross-country, with its nonstandard distances, challenging terrain, and team aspect, to be the perfect masters sport.

Kruell now focuses her season around cross-country. Although she can't help comparing her road or track times to previous marks, cross-country is about place. "Cross-country is all about running as hard as you can and beating as many people you can. That's satisfying," she said.

Not to mention the joy of getting dirty. "It is the greatest thing ever, out running in the mud," she said. "It is so much fun."

Cross-country adds the pleasure and satisfaction of competing with a team as well. "There is honor in being the fifth runner on any team," Kruell said. Time on the clock aside, she loves it most of all because, she said, "I get to run with my tribe."

As another team challenge, Kruell does relay events. She has run the Hood to Coast Relay for 20 of the last 22 years. "That's just running as hard as you can for no apparent reason," she said, smiling broadly. "It's the pure joy of running and being with a team. That's fun for me."

AGING THE CLOCK

Age groups, rivals, or team competitions provide satisfying, non-time-based goals for some masters as they adapt to changing realities. But what if you aren't motivated by social affirmation or head-to-head competition? For some, one of the attractions of running has always been that it isn't about beating someone else but rather about you versus you, measured by the clock.

What happens when the clock starts showing that rather than getting faster, you're getting worse while working harder?

Many lifetime competitors find motivation in having the clock age too—by applying age grading to times. Age grading is a method of adjusting times relative to age using formulas calculated by the World Masters Athletics association. These formulas, first published in 1989 and revised regularly, are based on decades of data on the best performances in every discipline at every age. Age-grading factors let you convert your time at any age to either a percentage of the world's best or an age-adjusted time theoretically equivalent to what you could run at your peak.

For example, when I race my local Fourth of July 5K every year, I can plug my time into an age-grading calculator and see that even though it may have been 10 seconds slower than last year, now that I'm a year older, it was an equivalent age-grading percentage. Or, I may discover that converted to an "open" time, it was better than I ever ran in my youth—an age-graded PR. Age grading gives us the chance to get better, even as we getting slower.

Former *Runner's World* editor Joe Henderson once called the tables "one of the most comforting books ever written on running." Many lifetime competitors tend to agree.

"Those of us who didn't start late, we really embrace age grading," Magill said. While masters who are new runners can still set lifetime bests, those who have PRs from youth have trouble getting excited about a time that they would have considered slow 10, 20, or 30 years ago. Those who ran world-class times in their youth, like Durden, find the converted times unattainable at their current age, but the tables do seem to accurately follow the aging curve for many.

"It's amazing how as I decline, how close the tables are," said Lang. "It's almost like it can predict how fast I'll run next year by plugging in the numbers and adding a year to my age." Lang says he has on occasion even made that his goal, to hit a time predicted by the age-graded calculator.

If you are motivated by competing with others, age grading can provide another benefit as well. By comparing percentages, you can compare your performance with anybody of any age or gender.

"Age grading has allowed me and Kathryn Martin to be rivals for 10 years," the 56-year-old Magill said. "In what other sport can I be archrivals with a 66-year-old woman?"

Of course, however scientifically it is compiled, age grading is a contrived device to help us stay motivated. We can't, nor should we, compare with others unless they too have bought into the concept. I've tried to compare my age-graded times with my teenage son and his high school cohorts' times, and they aren't buying it. They know they finished ahead of me in the race, and that is what is true and real today, not what I "could have" done at their age as calculated by some arcane formula. They are right, but there's no dishonesty in personally using age grading and enjoying the challenge of working toward these numbers.

"I love it, but it is a tool," Magill said. "We've made up all sorts of things." The adaptive challenge is to accept and believe the numbers for yourself as a way to scale effort and judge success.

I QUALIFIED

The quest to adapt our goals to our current level leads in different directions for every runner. In his youth, Griffin qualified for Boston several times, but never ran the race. Looking toward faster times, he never considered a Boston qualifier important. Today, in his mid-50s, he has arthritis in his knee that keeps him from training consistently. He's adapted his views so that now the goal of qualifying for Boston and being in Hopkinton on Patriots' Day motivates him to stretch himself and be the best he can within his current parameters. He never met the 50 to 54 standards, but he's recently joined the 55 to 59 age group and gained 10 more minutes.

Boston qualifying times are scaled to age, as are the standards to earn All-American status through USA Track and Field. These days, Mike Fanelli, 61, finds motivation in such scaling. Fanelli will sometimes check age grading after a race, but the conversions leave him cold. Perhaps because he ran so fast in his youth, he can't approach equivalent converted times now.

The All-American standards, however, keep him engaged, he said. "I'm always just on the cusp. For me, that's a really big reach to surpass and to qualify on the All-American standards."

The scalable standards seem appropriate to Fanelli. He always has to work to meet them, so they help him adapt to a new idea of what is a "good" time for a certain distance. "When you're in one age group, you can't wait to get to the next age group because you see what that standard is," he said. "Then every time you get to that age group, that time that seemed like a throwaway, you're like, 'This is really hard!'"

MAKING THE LIST

Some lifetime competitors reach a point when they find more meaning adopting goals that reward longevity. One example is trying to join the list of people who have run sub-3:00 marathons in five decades.

Such a list can be a strong motivator to keep chasing excellence for a few more years. Upon learning of the list, Mirth figured out that he already had three decades but needed to run one in the current decade, the 2010s, to make it four. He believes he might be able to hang on to get the fifth decade in the 2020s as well. "I'll only be 57 in 2020, so it should be well within my reach," he said. "Things that motivate me now are more longevity goals like that, since I can't do the speed thing anymore."

Those who have no hope of breaking 3:00 anymore (or ever) can consider goals that remove speed altogether. Early in 2017, Burfoot figured out that if he could finish Boston that spring, he would have completed a marathon in each of the seven decades of his life. He successfully completed the course, becoming, he believes, only the fifth person to have run a marathon in every decade from his teens to his 70s. Even someone as slow as me could conceivably join that list, having run a marathon in my teens, 20s, 30s, and 40s. Just the possibility added to my motivation to complete one in my 50s (which I did while writing this book), and it makes me look forward to my 60s and 70s.

STREAKS AND COLLECTING

For the past several years, Durden has kept himself motivated by what he calls "collecting." After being diagnosed with prostate cancer in 2003, he decided that running was still important to him and he wanted a goal to focus it around, something attainable even though he couldn't conceive of approaching the times of his youth or even age-graded equivalents.

"We got hooked on collecting marathons and running days," Durden told me when we met in a Boulder coffee shop. He and his wife, Amie, have now done a marathon in all 50 states and the District of Columbia and are on their second time around. Durden ran under 4:00 in all of them, even through cancer treatments. They brag about running 17 marathons in one calendar year, and Durden's total is now over 125 marathons.

For some, it might be too big a jump from making the Olympic team to collecting sub-4:00 marathons, but Durden sees it as congruous. He has defined his own competitiveness. "The pattern in all that [is that] I've been running," he said. "Even when I ran and I wasn't in really good shape, I always try to run as fast as I could given where I was. I never settled for 'This is just a fun run.'"

Even today, he relishes the head-to-head challenges within a race. "In the race, I'll pick out, say, an orange singlet, and I'll try to catch them," he said. "When I catch them, I'll look for another singlet."

As for Amie, while she used to be more competitive in her racing and training, she has adapted to a far more relaxed approach to running today. "I'm trying to be the best I can be on that given day," she said. "Every day is a PR, because you're one day older."

BEYOND RACING

For some lifetime competitors, racing doesn't hold their interest anymore. But although they don't compete, they still train toward goals. Their goals, however, tend to be very personal and often unscheduled. These goals are more about being fit and testing limits, away from comparisons and posted results.

"I seldom race," said Grimes. "Racing doesn't hold anything for me anymore." Racing was like playing a game for Grimes, he enjoyed the battles, but he finds that today he enjoys the process much more.

"I like to get in shape so I can still run," he said. "I don't need a race coming up to stay in shape. I need to stay in shape more for my mental well-being." Grimes still, however, has competitive drives. "I still like to see how fast I can run," he said.

For Douglas, beating others has never held much appeal, although he did plenty of it in his day. Putting in 150-mile weeks and hard speed work was what he enjoyed, and his racing was all about personal improvement, with the goals of running faster and being better than he had been before.

Racing itself became less appealing in his late 30s, however, when he realized he would never run those times again. "Once it was undeniable, I quickly lost interest in racing," Douglas said. He still appreciates the appeal of building and using fitness, of being able to say you did something well. But he finds racing has become disappointingly unpredictable. He can no longer rely on his body feeling a certain way on a given day, no matter what preparations and routines he follows.

Still, he trains like someone who has races on his schedule. But instead of trying to corral an unpredictable, aging body to a certain day, he runs hard when it tells him it is ready.

"Sometimes, it's a Wednesday. I feel good today, I'll go run," Douglas said. He'll do a half-hour tempo run, for example, and feel good about the effort and demonstrated skill. "To me, the race is today. I can get a large amount of that satisfaction on my own."

Douglas still cares about being fit and fast, but he doesn't feel a need to quantify it or compare with others. Rather, it is part of a daily process that defines and nourishes him. "Maybe at some point I will have to think, *What can I do to keep myself running?*" he said. "Now, it happens naturally."

WHY IT MATTERS

Having the ability to adapt your goals in order to match changing realities is essential to aging successfully. But being able to adapt goals to create an appropriate challenge matters from the first time we toe a start line, regardless of age.

Psychologist Carl Jung said that many difficulties can arise during the step from youth to adulthood. This is one of the life stages where runners often fall away. "No one can take the step into life without making certain assumptions, and occasionally these assumptions are false—that is, they do not fit the conditions into which one is thrown," Jung wrote in his essay "The Stages of Life." "Often it is a question of exaggerated expectations, underestimation of difficulties, unjustified optimism, or a negative attitude."

How often have you seen a high school runner discouraged because he or she didn't make varsity, or state, or receive a college scholarship? Even if they may have improved by a minute or more in the 5K, their exaggerated expectations or underestimation of the level of competition in their district doomed them to fail. In my experience, unjustified optimism is almost universal when it comes to college scholarship potential.

Expectations often lie at the center of whether we find joy or frustration in something, whether we get motivated and engaged or become negative and apathetic. Expectations inform our goals, and goals codify expectations.

Runners whose goals and dreams are rigid are likely to have them dashed. Griffin talked about how his unrealistic aspirations weighed on him during his most competitive years. "I look back now, at my decision to stop in my late 20s, and am convinced that a part of it at the time was that I was figuring out that I was never going to be as good as I wanted to be," Griffin said. "I was really struggling with that."

In hindsight, he believes the time constraints of becoming a father and his injury issues were actually just excuses to allow him to get out of the disappointment, to back away. Only later, when he could scale his goals to reality, was he able to come back to competition.

For another type of runner, rigid and limited goals fail to motivate beyond an early success. One runner whom I coached won state cross-country the fall of his senior year in high school and shut down soon after. He coasted through track his senior spring and underperformed for his first few years of college. He didn't train hard again until late in college, when he made it to nationals. As an adult, he's had an on-and-off relationship to running, seldom competing. His running goals have always been concrete, and as such, he had a difficult time scaling them to fit new realities or circumstances.

Successful lifetime competitors, in contrast, have found a variety of scalable goals that keep them working hard and trying to improve. Some of those goals, such as head-to-head age group competition, look a lot like their goals of youth, merely changing the comparison cohort. These goals depend on having the context of suitable rivals who can push them without frustrating them. In such a context, competing and winning create the same joy as they did at age 20.

Successful lifetime competitors have a variety of scalable goals that keep them working hard and trying to improve.

Other goals don't require the right context; they are infinitely variable to match a runner's current skill in order to motivate, produce flow, and enhance self-esteem. The wide variety of these goals shows not only the creativity of runners but also reveals emotional agility, the ability to adapt one's emotions to accept a different definition of what is "good."

WHAT SHOULD I DO TODAY?

Setting appropriate and adaptable goals starts with humility and honesty. A frank appraisal is required to assess both your current skill and the level of challenge that will bring out your best but not overwhelm.

For many of us, adapting goals as we age proves surprisingly difficult. In her book *Emotional Agility*, psychologist Susan David explains how we often get stuck because elements of our lives get hooked to emotions and we react to the emotion rather than rationally addressing the reality.

The emotion theory shines light on why runners get stalled or quit when adjusting goals and patterns. You can hear it in their language as they talk about times they run now, using words like *pathetic*, *embarrassing*, and *raging slow*. At some point, it seems, time ceased to be a neutral measurement of the ticks of a clock and got attached to judgments and emotions.

In the past, we could deal with negative emotions by working to change the reality—we could run harder and get in better shape. These emotions could be helpful because they motivated us to greater excellence. To have some contempt for a pace makes sense in the context of knowing one's potential and what can be done if the work is put in. It served us well to have some disgust for the temptation to settle for lazy.

When reality changes, however, our emotions often don't keep up. "People who are hooked into a particular way of thinking or behaving are not really paying attention to the world as it is," David wrote. "They're seeing the world as they've organized it into categories that may or may not have any bearing on the situation at hand."

Stepping Out

David suggests that the solution for dealing with an emotion-driven response is to create distance between reality and our response to it. There is nothing inherently fast or slow about a time.

Twenty years ago, 6:20 was a really good marathon pace for me. For the world's fastest marathoner, Eliud Kipchoge, that is an easy run. For others, it may be their best mile time. The point here is that a 6:20 time has no existential value outside of a context.

But today, when I run at what I think is a 6:20 level of effort and the clock reads 7:40, my initial reaction is shock and disappointment. And I'm discouraged and disgusted when I calculate my pace after a 5K and I discover it was only 6:30s. I feel like 6:30s should still be my "marathon pace" despite the fact that it is now my Vo_2max threshold. Emotions haven't kept up with reality.

Mirth talked about this type of emotional pairing in terms of training pace. "In my mind, 7-minute miles were always the separation between slow and fast for training," he said. "So I still carry that around with me today, if I can train under 7-minute miles, I've really been running."

His time barrier is entirely individual and arbitrary, yet it has stuck such that even now that he's adjusted his race goals and workout paces, he said, "I get aggravated if it is slower than about 7.5 minutes."

Emotions can also enter the picture when making comparisons with others. A careless comment can convince you that you should be ashamed of a race time. Emotional association often makes people run too fast on what should be easy days because they feel embarrassed to be seen running at a slower, more appropriate pace.

Just recognizing the emotions helps with moving on. David calls it "showing up," which involves awareness and acceptance. I heard this acceptance in the words of lifetime competitors. They acknowledged that getting slower was "depressing" and "demoralizing," that it "sucked," it was "no fun." They didn't deny these emotions; they simply separated them from how they reacted.

When you realize that you are reacting to a lifetime of associations with a certain pace or time, you create space between the emotion and the context. "This newly created space allows you to be sensitive to the context, to shift your actions to what will work in the here and now, rather than be driven by mindless impulses," David wrote. For the runner, this space allows you to see time in a larger context, as a neutral description of how fast you covered a distance, not good or bad, simply a tool you can use to assess your effort.

Emotional space also gives us emotional agility. You may fear that letting go of the emotional attachment to a time will leave you adrift and you'll lose your drive. But it can instead give you renewed motivation. Rather than feeling slow and getting slower, you can aim to be fast in a new context—"for someone this age." It isn't a cop-out. It is honesty. Think of it like living in a different country; the currency has a different value.

De Reuck's goals today are far distant from what they were, having once aimed for winning races and making Olympic teams. Today her goals include breaking 3:00 in the marathon or "having the miles in my legs to finish Comrades without walking this year."

She admitted that it took time to get to this place emotionally. But when I asked if goals like this could still motivate her, she said, "Yes, because it is a different era in [my] life." She has distanced herself from the emotion and placed herself in a new context.

Describing how his race goals have lowered, Mirth said, "You mentally adjust, and you forget the fact of what you used to be able to do."

Runners often resist such adjustments because our MO has always been to aim high and work until we get there. We have persistence, grit. It is our defining characteristic.

"It's easy to feel like a quitter if you're hooked on the idea that grit is a quality to be valued above all others," David wrote. "We should be gritty, but not stupid. The most agile and adaptive response to an unattainable goal is goal adjustment, which entails both disengaging from the unattainable goal and then reengaging in an alternative."

This is the path of successfully running through the decades, which involves giving up unattainable goals without giving up altogether. Instead, lifetime competitors reengage with alternative goals, goals that are still challenging but attainable.

Exploring

A useful tactic in adjusting your goals is to widen your variety of running challenges early in life. If you, as a road runner, do some of your training on steep, technical trails, you're unlikely to associate a pace that is 2 minutes per mile slower than your "regular" street pace with less effort or being lazy. Trying a new venue, like trail running or cross-country, introduces alternative goals instead of always trying to hit a certain time in standard distances. Or, go long: Run an ultramarathon where survival is paramount to speed.

Friend-Uhl credits her continued engagement with the sport partially to having a broad spectrum of goals. "I have a very big range," she said. "I can race everything from 400 m to the marathon and hold my own. I've always been more than just a track runner or a marathoner."

When one event or distance becomes stale or progress seems untenable, Friend-Uhl refocuses on building skills toward another. "There are plenty of goals to choose from," she said. "There's always something to work on."

At age 46, Friend-Uhl is still a relatively young master runner. At some point in her career, she will likely have to narrow her focus because she won't have the ability to train all the skills necessary for such a wide a range of races.

You can, however, switch to a new area and focus there at any age. Such a move will require that you develop new strengths. You will be starting over, with perhaps less initial success but also more opportunity for growth.

Creating Your Own Challenge

In addition to the variety of challenges the sport provides, you can make up your own. Like Benoit Samuelson, try creating stories around events and people in your life. It could be "Under 3-0 at 30" for the marathon (my personal goal in 1994) or under 5-0 at 50 in the mile; running a mile (or kilometer) for every life year on your birthday; hitting the year in miles, for example, 2,017 miles in 2017; or working up to a 50-mile or a 100-mile week. Yes, all these goals are arbitrary, but so is 26.2 miles. Their arbitrariness makes them personal and adaptable yet also challenging, if crafted to stretch you to expand your current ability.

Runners of any age can improve their ability to adapt by stepping back from exterior goals for periods without stepping back from running long and hard. Training at a similar intensity as you would if you had an upcoming race, without having a race that justifies the effort, allows you to focus on the pleasure and satisfaction of the act itself, of being fit and fast, of feeling alive, powerful, and young, no matter your age.

Douglas used the analogy of marriage to describe his changing relationship to running. "The most important things when you marry somebody aren't necessarily the basis of your relationship 20 to 25 years later," he said. "There's that underlying attraction that made you say, 'Wow, I love this.' Hopefully as circumstances change, you find new things that produce that 'Wow' feeling."

THE EARLY MARATHON

One surprise among lifetime competitors' stories was discovering how many had run a marathon or ultra early in life, often in high school. I ran my first marathon at age 16 and always thought I was unique, but instead found that about half of those I met, still chasing it at 50-plus, had also gone long early.

One explanation might be the era. Many of these runners came of age when running was young, people were crazy, and everyone was doing the marathon. If you were "serious," you went long.

Whatever the reason, it seems that an early marathon may well have provided a few benefits for these runners that influenced them to continue in the sport. One was that it linked them to a world of open, individual running beyond high school and college so that when school ended, the road forward as a runner was obvious. The marathon also gave young runners knowledge that the road ahead held plenty of challenges and a world of competitors, many of whom were better than them. And it introduced them to the fact that some competitors were even "old" men and women.

Success in the marathon also weighs experience and training more heavily than natural ability, thus encouraging and rewarding persistence. Many had a difficult experience in their first marathon and were able to improve dramatically as they learned to train for the distance. Even so, marathon success is elusive—more can go wrong, and with larger consequences, than in a 5K—thus enticing runners to keep working toward an optimal effort.

Finally, related to emotional agility, learning the broad range of running challenges may have helped keep running times from getting too closely categorized. If you race everything from the 800 m to the marathon, you have to have some sense of context, even within your own efforts. You learn that whether a given pace is "good" or "bad" has to be in context. The answer is always "it depends."

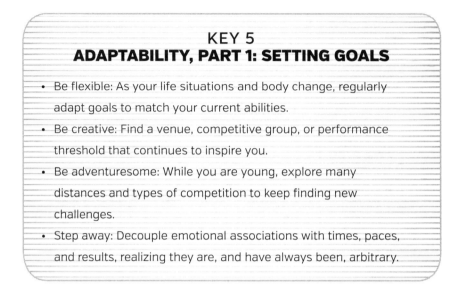

KEY 5
ADAPTABILITY, PART 1: SETTING GOALS

- Be flexible: As your life situations and body change, regularly adapt goals to match your current abilities.
- Be creative: Find a venue, competitive group, or performance threshold that continues to inspire you.
- Be adventuresome: While you are young, explore many distances and types of competition to keep finding new challenges.
- Step away: Decouple emotional associations with times, paces, and results, realizing they are, and have always been, arbitrary.

7

ADAPTABILITY, PART 2
FLEXING WITH THE TIMES

> We cannot live the afternoon of life according to
> the program of life's morning, for what was great in the morning
> will be little at evening and what in the morning was true,
> at evening will have become a lie.
>
> —CARL JUNG, "THE STAGES OF LIFE"

Training and goals are so intertwined, it's hard to tell which comes first. Do we adapt new goals to new training realities or adapt training patterns to new goals? Regardless, adapting both is essential when it comes to surviving and thriving through the decades.

Lifetime competitors all train differently today than they did in high school or when chasing PRs in their 20s and 30s. Even as masters, training changes year by year, season by season. These training adaptations may be driven by changes in life situations, competitive goals, health, or age. This chapter focuses on strategies runners use to help them adapt and succeed in the face of these changes, particularly aging.

MILES TO GO BEFORE I SLEEP

Adapting to age, generally speaking, involves going from more to less. "I used to do XX miles per week, now I only do XX," runner after runner told me. The numbers they cited varied widely; much depends on where people started, what their goals are presently, what their preferences are, and how healthy they have stayed. I did not come away from my interviews with definitive guidance such as "cut down 10 percent for every decade." But some patterns did emerge after hearing from more than 50 runners.

One finding is that while runners' ability to handle miles differs, one hundred–plus miles a week is a lot for any human, and few runners maintain this high of mileage into their masters years. Those who once did 100-, 120-, or 140-mile weeks now tend to run 60 to 80. To be sure, that's still a lot of miles, more than most recreational runners do in their youth, but it is a big reduction.

Some who never topped 60 to 80 continue to maintain that level without injury. It seems that runners don't have to reduce their volume arbitrarily if their volume wasn't pushing the limits before they started aging.

Ruben is a model of consistent marathoning, running in the 2:30s to 2:50s for decades. He kept the same level of miles throughout his 50s— 70 to 80 miles a week—which he still maintains even after having a stroke. "My mileage never got that high," Ruben said. "I always thought I could do more miles if I had more time or was more aggressive. But I wanted to be healthy and not force it."

Several others with lower total volume, such as 40 to 50 miles per week, have maintained this volume as they aged. Those who have reduced beyond this point have done so because of time constraints or a desire for more rest days between hard sessions, not because of volume-induced injuries.

A second observation is that having the discipline to run the easy miles at an appropriate pace is at least as important as the number of miles put in. Runners tend to get stuck in a rut regarding what is an acceptable, comfortable pace, and they often fail to adjust as that changes. These are the ones who seem most likely to get injured by the volume.

"The biggest challenge is not the impossibility of doing the volume," Paulk said. "The challenge is slowing down to do the volume, slowing down the pace." This can result in reduced miles simply because of the time constraints.

STILL GOING LONG

While many maintain that intensity is more important than volume as you age, it seems that those who continue to perform at the highest level as masters continue to do volume as well. None of the lifetime competitors I talked to, not even track runners, had eschewed daily runs and long runs completely and replaced them with all-out intensity, à la CrossFitters.

Benoit Samuelson has done high miles for decades. Today she puts in approximately 60 to 75 per week. "Higher mileage weeks usually start three months out from a targeted marathon," she said. She supplements these with 20 or more miles of Nordic skiing in the winter and cycling in the summer. Other lifetime runners reported similar mileage totals, as much as 70 to 80 per week, well into their 60s.

Whitlock was another example of high-volume success, if on the extreme end of the spectrum. He estimated his weekly total while marathon training at age 70 to be near 140 miles per week. (It's important to note that Whitlock did not put in big miles in his youth.)

Whether these exceptional athletes run so well because they do the miles or they can do the miles because they run so well is uncertain. Regardless, the secret to running success for masters as well as youth is certainly tied at least in part to distance.

QUALITY CONTROL

When it comes to speed, successful masters runners still train fast regularly. Unlike less-competitive masters who tend to avoid intensity for fear of injury, top competitors continue to get in intense workouts. These may be more informal sessions than before, but successful masters push it once or twice a week and make sure it is quality work.

"A lot of masters think you should never do speed work. I don't fall into that camp," said Sperandeo. "I still believe in speed."

Since becoming a master, Kastor said that "trying to keep up with the quality of the workouts has been the focus."

While they do tough workouts, masters report that they do less volume of intensity. Some reduce volume by going by feel. Others have applied more specific step-down strategies.

Mirth figured out that he was more likely to do workouts if he kept the volume low. "I limit myself," Mirth said. He keeps the total of his intense workouts to around 1.5 miles, no more than 2 miles. If he's doing a 400m workout, for example, he limits it to 6 repeats, down from what once was 12 to 16. "I don't think I would have survived as long if I was still running 4 × 1 mile all out, or 16 × 400," he said. "I find I don't need to run that kind of volume. I can still race at an equal level on the shorter speed work."

Grimes has adopted a similar approach in his 50s but frames it differently. "I try to get one and a half hard workouts a week, and a long run. And the other times, it is just recovery runs," he said.

What is a half-workout? Essentially, he still does two workouts a week, but reduces each workout by about a third.

"In college, we would do 20 400s or 12 800s," Grimes explained. "Now, I might do 4 or 5 800s. Instead of doing 6 1-mile repeats, I'll do 4. When you add it up, that is a hard workout and a half in a week, rather than two hard workouts."

AS GOOD AS I ONCE WAS

Champion 56-year-old middle-distance runner Paulk said that while he, like others, does less volume now, the intensity remains the same for his all-out track work. He can't go as fast, but he works just as hard.

What has changed for him is the number and frequency of workouts. Whereas up until his 30s he would put in three hard workouts a week with one recovery day in between, now he runs two hard workouts per week and needs two to three recovery days after each. And, unlike in the past, he takes a day off every week or two.

Similarly, Friend-Uhl, who is in her mid-40s, noted that for her the biggest change and challenge is the need for more recovery. She has close to the same speed as she used to and she can crank out aggressive sessions, but afterward she finds that she can't come back and do another one very quickly.

"In my head, I'm still 25, and I'm willing to work that hard and that aggressively, but my body can't handle that anymore," she said. "I need more rest days in between, more recovery runs between workouts."

Paulk's and Friend-Uhl's adjustments highlight one change on which masters athletes and researchers agree: namely, the need to reduce the density of your training. In his book *Fast After 50*, coach Joe Friel makes an important distinction between training dose and training density. Dose is how hard any one session is; density is how frequently you administer that dosage.

"Both dose and density need to decrease as age increases," Friel said. But distinguishing between the two helps guide that reduction and explains why aging athletes find that while they can run just as hard and nearly as fast as ever, they get in trouble if they try to do so very frequently. Or, as country singer Toby Keith put it, "I'm as good once as I ever was."

Friel explains it in less colorful terms. "We can generally do a high-dose session, perhaps even as hard as when we were much younger, but we can't do several of them in a few days' time," he wrote. "While both dose and density are concerns of the senior athlete, I've found the density becomes the one that gives us the most trouble as we get older."

In *IronFit's Marathons After 40*, Don and Melanie Fink explain this in a formula:

$$\text{Training Volume} = \text{Duration} \times \text{Intensity} \times \text{Frequency}$$

Like Friel, they agree that frequency is often the most important variable in this equation when adapting workouts for masters runners.

NARROWING THE FIELD

Partly as a result of not being able to work as hard as often, masters tend to specialize as they move into higher age groups. Some focus on new challenges where they can see growth and avoid comparisons with prior times. Many, however, return to the part of the sport they enjoy the most and events that take advantage of what they do best. Either way, the constraints of reduced volume and greater recovery times require that they no longer try to do everything.

Paulk and Benson ran marathons after college, but both came back to middle-distance track as masters. When he was approaching 50, Benson decided to shoot for a sub-5:00 mile. He felt that the road mileage he was putting in while training for marathons was aging his legs prematurely.

"*I'm a middle-distance runner,*" he recalled thinking. "*I should go back to my strengths.*" He found he enjoyed it, had success, and has since focused exclusively on middle-distance track.

In this narrowing, you can't follow anyone else's pattern; you have to find what is right for you. Bailey dabbled in road racing, but now, in his 50s, he focuses on races shorter than a mile. "It's a shame that more people don't run track," Bailey said. From his perspective, short and fast is better for aging runners. In contrast, however, Mark Buciak focuses on the marathon. He has never liked speed and finds the hardest races are those under 5 miles. "It's in my DNA," Buciak said. "I don't get warmed up until about the 15-mile mark."

SELECTIVE OPTIMIZATION

Reducing the range of your running matches with theories of successful aging. In their book *Successful Aging*, the Balteses call this process "selective optimization."

They define *selection* as "an increasing restriction of one's life world to fewer domains." We can't do everything anymore, we can't fit it all in and recover enough to improve and stay healthy, thus we tend to focus on specific areas. These areas, the Balteses say, "involve a convergence of environmental demands and individual motivations, skills and biological capacity." In other words, we focus on the areas we like and we can do well.

The benefit of such selection is that we can improve in those areas even if our overall capacity is reduced. The Balteses called this "optimization," in which people continue to "enrich and augment" their ability and "maximize their chosen life courses." Not having to do 20-milers for an upcoming marathon and thus fitting in another speed workout, for example, helps a miler get better.

"As you age, you have to pick," Benson said. "What am I going to do? Should I not run as hard, should I not run as fast, should I not run as often, should I not run as far?" You can't do every element you need to be fit for any distance.

Not reducing your range of focus can spell disaster. Consider Mike Spinnler's story. His first love was ultramarathoning. He ran the JFK 50 Mile as a teenager, eventually winning it at age 24 and setting the course record. He was running at the top of his game.

"Then, I tried to do too many things," he said. "I'd only run one ultra a year, and one marathon. But I tried to run on the track as well. By trying to do intense speed along with high-volume stuff, I tore my Achilles tendon in a 5000m race."

The tear required three surgeries, and while Spinnler continued to run, running was never quite the same again, he said. The Achilles problem led to knee problems, which eventually led to Spinnler being a cyclist and a coach—and no longer a runner.

MAINTENANCE MODE

Another area of training where masters tend to adapt involves the supplemental or complementary work around running: stretching, strengthening, drills. What each runner needs in this area differs wildly, but unless you are supremely gifted, what you need will increase as you age.

Some lifetime competitors scoffed when asked if they did supplementary work. "I don't do any of that stuff," Erickson said. "I don't stretch, I don't do core stuff. I can't stand to lift weights."

Ruben avoids it as well. "I do the barest amount of stretching before I go out running. About a minute," he said.

Several said it wasn't worth taking away from miles on the road. "That's all time that could be spent running," Dunham said. Mirth agreed. "I invest my time in my running instead of other work," he said.

Many, however, have found the extra work necessary as they age.

As for me, I was a late convert (after 45) to core strength and flexibility work. My research convinced me that it is necessary to counteract the effect of decades of sitting and hunching, and my experience revealed that it has made my stride lighter and given me the ability to run more miles with fewer injuries.

Other lifetime competitors echoed this experience. Pillin started doing core work in his late 40s. "Core exercises helped me to be a lot more fit overall than the skinny runner I used to be," Pillin said. "I think they are helping the longevity of my career."

In her youth, Kruell did drills and weights as part of competitive teams, but she got away from it in her 30s. Today, in her late 50s, she's back at them after injuries provided a wake-up call. She now works on balance and hip strength regularly.

"As you get older, your form starts to deteriorate," Kruell said. "You wind up getting injured because you're not using your body properly."

Fanelli said he didn't do much extra work in his youth because he didn't need it as much, and runners didn't know as much back then. That has changed. Today, at 61, he said he is in perpetual "maintenance mode."

"My focus is first and foremost on the recovery phase," he said. "I may only run 40 minutes to an hour a day, but I spend another one and half or two hours doing all the ancillary stuff."

Fanelli considers adapting to this kind of work one of the dividers between those who continue running for decades and those who stop. "Most people aren't willing to do that. None of it is fun," he said. The way to get your mind around it, he believes, is to think of the challenge of dealing with aging body parts and systems as part of the training and racing puzzle. Paying attention to what you can and cannot do becomes the core challenge, Fanelli said. "You just have to understand what you can do to maximize fitness while looking after the damage and trying to keep the damage from expanding."

Douglas, too, has found he's had to up his maintenance work as he's aged, and like Fanelli, he sometimes spends more time on extra stuff than he does running. Douglas does a variety of supplementary exercises: TheraBand single-leg balance work, step overs, push-ups, and core exercises. He suspects that ignoring these extras is a big reason people give up the sport as masters. "It gets physically harder for everybody," he said. "But a lot of people don't care for their bodies, so it gets harder faster, and soon it is not going to feel good to run."

He recognizes that most runners would rather be out on the road and track, and furthermore, they don't think of running as related to their overall health. But he's adamant about doing the supplemental work. "Why not put yourself in a position to run better?" he said.

Adam Chase, a 51-year-old longtime runner from Boulder who is well known on the trail running scene, does about six hours a week of gym work but doesn't consider it as onerous as do many lifetime masters. Perhaps this is because he started doing such work early in life, even in high school, so it is a normal part of his routine. In addition, he said he sets challenges for himself in the gym, such as how much he can bench-press or how many pull-ups he can do, and finds this motivating and engaging. His goal—to be overall fit, not just running fit—differs from many lifetime competitors, who tend to see anything outside of running as a distraction. But it has served him well, allowing him to adapt and thrive into the years when overall fitness becomes a key part of being able to continue as a runner.

EXPERIMENTATION AND EVOLUTION

As with other parts of training, the extras required to enhance your running will be different for every runner. Furthermore, those requirements will evolve, and so require adaptation.

How do we know what our personal limits are, where we need to focus, where and how much we need to cut back? By paying attention and experimenting. As discussed in Chapter 4, successful masters run by feel, constantly monitoring and adapting their training based on how their body and mind respond.

Lots of runners adhere to George Sheehan's assertion that we are "each an experiment of one" and discover through this experiment what works for them. Unfortunately, many then stick with one pattern—the one that worked, that once brought them success—even when it no longer applies.

This is not just a problem among runners. "The nearer we approach to the middle of life . . . the more it appears as if we had discovered the right course and the right ideals and principles of behavior," Jung wrote in "The Stages of Life." "For this reason we suppose them to be eternally valid, and make a virtue of unchangeably clinging to them."

We have to keep experimenting, and the time frame in which the results remain valid reduces with each passing year. You may have figured out what works for you at 20, and that remained true for a decade. But what you discover works at 50 may only be applicable until you are 52.

Jung continued on the dangers of assuming you have the answers as you step into the second half of life. "Thoroughly unprepared, we take the step into the afternoon of life," he wrote. "Worse still, we take this step with the false presupposition that our truths and our ideals will serve us as hitherto."

Magill echoed Jung as he discussed training into the masters years. "The things you will understand at 55 that you don't understand at 51 are beyond your comprehension," Magill said. "The things you can do at 55 are not the things you could do at 50—forget 40." The solution is constant experimentation, Magill said, "a constant reshuffling of athletic and training priorities and trying to make it all fit, and still end up with a good product."

TRAMPLE ON THE PAST

How do we step away from patterns that worked? How do we move away from the emotional attachment to paces and totals that have told us what is "good" and motivated us to greater accomplishments? One strategy that emerged as I talked to lifetime competitors was to work to forget.

It is a strategy echoed in the world's great literature. "What makes old age hard to bear is not the failing of one's faculties, mental and physical, but the burden of one's memories," W. Somerset Maugham wrote in his memoir, *The Summing Up*.

How do we deal with those memories and move on? "We have to learn to trample on the past," V. S. Naipal wrote in his novel *A Bend in the River*. He was talking about major movements in history, transformations of countries and cultures, but his advice applies as well to the changes in one's lifetime. "It isn't easy to turn your back on the past," he warned. "It is something you have to arm yourself for, or grief will ambush and destroy you."

Sperandeo trampled on the past in dramatic fashion. At age 37, he was hit by a drunk driver while running and broke his femur at the knee and hip. It took him over a year to walk and longer still to be able to run. So when he turned 40 and felt ready to start running competitively again, he needed to start over.

"First thing I did, [I] took all my old diaries and threw them away," he said. "I didn't box them up, didn't pack them for later. I threw them in the garbage can."

The act of throwing out the logs freed him to create new training patterns and set new goals. "I started new, and everything I did was a PR," he said.

Sperandeo did the same thing when he turned 50. This time, he was recovering from cancer and radiation treatment. Throwing out everything from his 40s, he started over again.

He thinks every runner should throw out his or her logs at the start of a new decade. "Your first workout when you turn 50, you do 400s, that's your PR," he said. "See if you can break that next time."

Other lifetime competitors talked about trampling on the past by no longer tracking miles or keeping logs at all.

"That's fantastic information to have if you're training to race," Grimes said. "But for now, my interest is to run what I can run and be happy with it—and not worry about what I was doing last week and not compare to what I was doing a year ago."

My interest is to run what I can run and be happy with it.
–DANIEL GRIMES

It's intentional self-delusion, but perhaps easier than keeping the past close and constantly trying to separate emotions from the times and totals. Those can exist in the past and in our minds while we run today and enjoy the feeling without having to quantify it.

"Obviously I care—I don't want to get slower," Grimes admitted. "But if I don't keep track, then I don't know how much slower I'm getting."

CTRL/ALT/DELETE

Many masters runners described distinct resets in their running life. Most are not as drastic as Sperandeo's, but these moments often did involve injury and a time of rebuilding from zero.

Magill has had several reboots, described in Chapter 2. A few were lifestyle driven, where he got away from the sport and had to start again. Others were smaller resets, when he has taken time away from running and given himself permission to try new patterns.

Several lifetime competitors experienced a similar reset around injuries. Following several strong running years in his 40s, where he ran nearly the same times every race, near the top in the world for his age, Paulk's feet fell apart at 48. He tried everything to get rid of his plantar fasciitis, including surgery, while still trying to do the same training he had always done. He finally had to drop back to zero and restart.

"It took years of injury, surgery, rehab to finally get really frustrated, to say, 'This is not just a once-in-a-while thing, it is going to keep reoccurring unless you do something different. It is not going to go away unless you change,'" Paulk explained.

Today he's working on finding a new pattern of training, the right volume, the right density, and all the extras needed to keep him healthy and rebuilding. "Some people don't get to the reset. I got to the reset; I'm in the reset mode," he said.

Dr. Mark Cucuzzella calls it doing a "Ctrl/Alt/Delete"—the process of rebooting and starting at zero. A 2:24 marathoner with recurrent injuries, he had foot surgery at age 34 to repair chronic arthritis in his toes and was told he would not compete again.

He used the occasion to rediscover how to run again, this time without shoes. He started with walking, then slowly running across the driveway, then down the block, learning how to move and building new strengths. Today, at age 51, he's able to run marathons in the 2:30s.

At some point, many runners require a reset back to zero. They need to ditch their current routine—not try to maintain a certain mileage, not hit certain splits or perform tried-and-true workouts—and start over, unburdened by old expectations and habits.

BC/AD

The arrival of children also prompted a reset for many.

Benoit Samuelson said the biggest change in her running came when her kids were born in 1988 and 1991. She refers to the evolution as BC/AD: Before Children and After Diapers. "I used to schedule my day around my running before I had kids, when I was at the top of my game," she said. "Since having kids, I've always scheduled my running around my day."

When Kastor failed to make the marathon team in the 2012 Olympic Trials, she felt the need for a reset. Her daughter Piper had been born a few months before, and Kastor had worked training around being a mother. "I felt really discouraged," she said. "I felt I had failed as a runner and as a parent. It was the first time my attention was needed elsewhere, besides training. I needed to figure out how to make them coexist."

She reset her priorities, putting family first. Note that she still recognizes that she is a runner and competitor. "It was really good to set those priorities," she said. "But it also made me realize that sometimes those lines aren't as distinct as they seem, because sometimes getting out to run makes you a better parent and makes you healthier."

=

WHY IT MATTERS

Adapting isn't an option; it is a necessity for survival. "Adapt or die" is so commonly used it is a cliché. Failure to adapt is a common reason runners fall away from the sport. Life changes and their training, habits, and goals don't adjust in response.

> *Adapting isn't an option; it is a necessity for survival.*

Runners leave high school or college and no longer have a team, a coach, or a convenient daily training schedule. They move, change jobs, have kids, get injured. A training partner moves or the Sunday-morning group run falls apart. Even if none of this happens, eventually runners get older and abilities change.

To adapt, runners at any age can work to develop flexible habits and avoid rigid ruts. Running at the same time every day is common among runners and is certainly useful in establishing an automatic habit. If this becomes the *only* way you will run, however, what happens when your schedule changes and you're not able to run at that time?

The same is true for training patterns and plans. Getting stuck on the idea that "this is what I have to do" can create trouble when you no longer can do that. Latching on to one coach or philosophy that makes sense to you and works is certainly part of the "experiment of one" process, and thus is useful and necessary to refine how your body reacts to training. But it can also lead to staleness. In a 2014 *Runner's World* column, Alex

Hutchinson wrote, "Every training plan, no matter how well thought out, becomes less effective if you do the same things week after week and year after year. Your body responds most strongly to unfamiliar stimuli, and after prolonged repetition even the toughest workouts suffer from the law of diminishing returns." He advised that you regularly change variables in your training simply for the sake of change. "Sometimes the magic is the change itself," Hutchinson said.

WHAT SHOULD I DO TODAY?

Mixing things up at all points in your life will make it easier to introduce variety when you actually have to. Variety helps you get the most out of yourself and avoid injury. And by constantly changing some variable, you might find that a new pattern works even better. (Just don't stop experimenting; remember, something else might work better tomorrow.)

More than any one thing you can do, however, developing adaptability requires adopting certain mindsets. Similar to the emotional agility needed to change goals, becoming free to train differently requires acknowledging and releasing the emotional attachments to tried-and-true practices and patterns.

As discussed in Chapter 4, runners often attach emotions to a certain mileage, number of speed workouts, type and intensity of workouts, splits hit during each. If we can't hit a minimum amount of miles a week, we feel like we're no longer runners. We feel disappointment and frustration if we can't crush the workouts we once could.

Fanelli says it's a challenge for many runners, including himself, to adjust their perspectives. "Can we handle the altered expectations?" he asked. "Because it is embarrassing to train as hard as I do and to run as slow as I do compared to the past."

He said a lot of runners his age could still be out there running if they wanted to, "but are they willing to do all they can to leverage stuff, are they willing to be in that management mode?" Fanelli shrugged. "I think it is largely our egos. We can't wrap our heads around training this hard to run that slow—slower than our warm-up paces! I can't run one mile at my marathon pace, not one, and I train hard!"

Becoming free to train differently requires
acknowledging and releasing the emotional attachments
to tried-and-true practices and patterns.

Note Fanelli still called it his "marathon pace"—not his former pace or best pace. Once a certain performance level is achieved, runners often add it to their identity. They say, "I'm a [fill in time]-hour marathoner," not "I've run a marathon in [fill in time]." Losing that reality doesn't imply just a change in our goals and training but in our identity. It's a tough place to be, but Fanelli accepts the challenge.

"It helps to be able to philosophize one's way to this place of acceptance," Fanelli said. "Of being where you're at and being comfortable and confident with where you're at. Then maximizing it."

Not Just a Blip

Another reason we sometimes have trouble adapting to a new reality is that our performance level was never static in the first place. We work for years to build up to our top level, always feeling that we can improve if we work harder.

Friend-Uhl described a scenario familiar to many. When coming back from an injury soon after she became a masters runner, she said, "I remember just being frustrated. I kept thinking: *It's going to come back, it's going to come back*—but it wasn't."

Judd Esty-Kendall, a 67-year-old competitor from Bangor, Maine, described taking a year to come back from Achilles surgery in his early

60s. "A lot of it was my fault," he said. "Trying to come back too early. You think it is just a little blip in the road, and it was more than that."

Runners are used to seeing an obstacle as merely another challenge that they need to work to overcome. Indeed, optimism is a key characteristic of lifetime competitors and is examined closely in Chapter 10. But optimism, while imperative, must not keep us from adapting to reality. An important tool to help us distinguish between mere blips and permanent changes is honesty.

Listen to the Truth

Will Lindgren talks a lot about honesty. A lifetime runner and coach in Omaha, Nebraska, Lindgren has founded and led several elite and sub-elite teams through the years. He believes the key to aging well is to reconcile reality with dreams and aspirations.

"If you can cross that bridge," Lindgren said, "that takes you into the golden twilight of running." But he says the only way you can cross that bridge is with honesty, and that means accepting your level of fitness and skill today—not where you want to be, not where you once were, but where you are now.

Lindgren ties honesty to effort, which doesn't change no matter your age or ability. You know where you are, Lindgren said, "if you can finish a workout and say, 'I did my best.'"

"Your best" is the hardest challenge there is, even harder than competing with others, because it allows no room for winning easy. Similarly, you could run a best time, and if it wasn't your best effort, you're not really competing.

Lindgren separates success from time or place. The focus is on honesty and effort. "If you're racing your best against yourself, you're always going to feel like a winner," he said. "You've acquitted yourself with pride and honesty. That gives you the sense of accomplishment."

Making effort your guide and goal removes the fear many have of decoupling emotion from measurements and ending up adrift and unmotivated. We want to stay attached to measures of excellence. But rather than feeling disappointment when we don't hit a certain split, we can note when we weren't really focused and tough. If we're honest about the effort, we can remain just as passionate, we can push just as hard and celebrate excellence—but excellence tied to a flexible, adaptable standard.

Judging workouts and races by effort returns us to the idea of running by feel, explored in Chapter 4. Learn to judge efforts apart from the times you achieved early in your running career, when you could rely on times to reflect certain paces and provide feedback. Because when that correlation starts to change, you don't want to doubt the level of effort.

Fifty-three-year-old Chris Zenker described a scene I heard from many. "You put that effort in, and you look at your clock. Five years ago it would have been one number," Zenker said. "You look at it now and go, 'Really? The effort was there, that can't be that slow!'"

Friend-Uhl described doing speed work after she turned 40. "It's hard because you're in a workout and you're not sure, was that a good workout or not?" she said. "It was hard to read my body. It took about a year to get there."

If you haven't been tuning in so that you know and trust the effort, you're likely to run harder to match the time. And you're likely to get hurt doing your workouts too fast or discouraged because the effort is too much to be fun anymore.

Letting go of arbitrary and rigid goals and training patterns—and the emotions attached to them—sets you free to listen when your body tells you it needs to rest and when it is ready to go hard. And every day, easy or hard, learn to let the effort dictate the intensity and the success of the run.

The effort is ageless.

The Freedom of Loneliness

One practical way to enhance your adaptability is to learn to run alone. Nearly all the runners I interviewed said that they run most of their miles by themselves. They cite a number of reasons, from enjoying the solitude to building mental toughness, but the reason it is essential to lifetime competitors, however, appears to be primarily because it frees the runner to adapt to changing life situations and abilities.

Benoit Samuelson mostly runs alone and always has. "Even when I was at the top of my game, most of my running was done on my own," she said. She links going it alone to training by feel. By herself, she can decide how far and how fast. She is able to listen to and respond to her own body rather than to other runners, and adapt the workout at will rather than going along with the group or negotiating a change in plans.

Emery also likes running alone because she can set her own pace. "When you're with somebody else, you have to go faster, faster, faster . . . pretty soon you're flying along," Emery said. "I enjoy running alone better."

Lang does more running alone now that he's older, for the freedom of solitude. "I've kind of become a lone wolf. I do 98 percent of my running now alone," he said. "The older I get, the more I just do what I want to do."

That freedom to do what you want also includes scheduling. "I've always liked the ability to leave my door, come back, be home—I waste zero time," Lang said.

Erickson echoed this. "I'm a loner," she said. "It is just too hard to get everybody scheduled."

Scheduling, traveling, and waiting on others adds to the time commitment that is often already precariously close to overloading runners' availability.

Then there are the number of miles and the difficulty of finding someone who is willing to do them with you.

Edward Abbey wrote in *Desert Solitaire*, "Most of my wandering in the desert I've done alone. Not so much from choice as from necessity—I generally prefer to go into places where no one else wants to go."

Such is the case for many runners. No one close by wants to go as far or as often as we do. Which is fine: Like Abbey, we're happy to go it alone.

"I've probably run more by myself," Rodgers said. "You've got to remember, I was running twice a day from age 26 to [my] late 40s, 50."

This seems to get worse with age. "These days, almost every single run I do is alone. There's no one to train with," Magill said. "At my age, there just aren't runners left who are doing the kind of training I am."

He'd train with the younger guys, he said, but he can't match their accelerations during speed work. They end up 30 yards ahead by the time he gets up to speed, and even though he then matches their pace, they're no longer running together. And on long runs, he said he's slowed down too much for others to want to run with him. Running solo is the only way he can adapt to his current needs in volume, intensity, and density of training.

Seeking Company, Sometimes

That said, many lifetime competitors do seek out company at times. Many find they prefer to be alone on easy days and to run with others on workout days where, if they're lucky enough to join others of similar ability, they are inspired to greater efforts.

Buciak prefers a combination. "There are days when I want to be with a group of people to pull me along, or for socialization. There are days just to retreat, and I want to run by myself," he said.

Robinson also praised a mixture. "I'm very happy running on my own," he said. "But I've also loved the friends I made."

All agreed, however, that regardless of preference, a runner simply must be able to run alone or he or she won't make it as a lifetime runner.

"If you can't run alone, if you depend on a buddy, you'll have difficulty," Robinson said. "You need to be self-driven."

"I don't prefer to be alone, but I can get the job done if I am," Friend-Uhl said. "I don't need people around me to support me."

Benoit Samuelson pointed out that when life changes, you can't depend on others to provide your motivation. "When you move away or can't keep up or a group falls apart, then what do you do?" she said.

Those who haven't learned to train alone often fall away after leaving a school team. Those who depend on a training partner too often lose the habit when the fragile relationship ends: one person's schedule changes, one partner gets injured, one changes goals or sports, or you find you're aging at different rates.

Learning to run alone is one of the simplest and most practical ways to ensure that you keep going for a lifetime. Becoming a solo runner helps facilitate many of the principles in this book: consistency, flexible variety, training by feel, and most of all, adaptability.

KEY 5
ADAPTABILITY, PART 2:
FLEXING WITH THE TIMES

- Build adaptive skills: Mix up your training to become comfortable with multiple patterns, develop your ability to train by feel, and learn to love running alone.
- Run hard less often: Successful aging runners maintain volume and intensity but reduce the density of training.
- Trample on the past: To adapt new training patterns, let go of what you could once do, reset, and focus on being your best today.
- Specialize and optimize: As recovery takes more time so that you can no longer fit in as much training, narrow the range of events you run and do more specific training to optimize them.

8

STUDENTS OF THE SPORT
KNOWLEDGE THAT DIRECTS AND EXCITES

The man armed with knowledge has a better chance
of survival than the man who is simply the fittest.
Knowledge is the true strength. Muscle is where the myth is.

–SUZY KASSEM, *RISE UP AND SALUTE THE SUN*

Halfway through my interviews, I had formulated an idea that one of the keys to longevity was self-coaching. I mentioned this to Mike Spinnler, one of the later interviews, but he, a coach himself, objected. Spinnler believes in the importance of coaching to motivate and support, and thus he saw having a coach as a benefit, not a detriment. And indeed, as interviews progressed, I learned that many lifetime competitors either have coaches now or had good coaches at key points in their lives.

What I realized was contributing to these competitors' success and longevity was not the absence of a coach but rather the presence of the runners' own deep knowledge. It became clear that in order to survive and thrive, you must be a student of the sport. This means knowing not only how training works and what types of training are effective to prepare for different races, but also how your own body reacts to training. In other words, you need both theory and lab work.

HEAD TO THE LIBRARY

"I've always been a student of the sport," Friend-Uhl said, articulating what I heard from virtually every runner. "If we're going to dedicate ourselves to something, we have a responsibility to do our best at it, and so to understand what we're doing and why it is very important."

Many were this way from the beginning. Robinson had to learn how to train himself because he was in a school setting where runners simply formed a club and didn't have a coach. Others, like Mirth, had a coach, but not one who knew the sport. "My coaches the first two and a half years of high school were basically football coaches," Mirth said. "We were left to ourselves to figure out what to do for training."

Others became students as adults, when they found themselves on their own and wanted to improve. Runner after runner told me they read voraciously on the topic, from classic training texts by Cerutty, Elliott, Lydiard, Bowerman, and others to *Runner's World* and other periodicals. I remember in high school writing a paper on Dr. Dave Costill's carbo-loading research, which I had to access from scholarly journals borrowed by interlibrary loan. I, like so many others, learned all I could and then formulated my own synthesized philosophy and program. For lifetime competitors, this hunger to learn never waned; reading and learning continued up to the present day.

MENTORS

Not all had to start on their knowledge journey alone. Many credit a mentor for setting them on the path to learning.

Kruell arrived at the beginning of the women's cross-country program at Cornell and found the coaching inadequate. "You really had to figure out what you needed to do," she said.

Lucky for Kruell, budding physiologist Pete Pftizinger was a senior when she was a freshman. Pfitzy, who would go on to win the Olympic

Trials and become a coach, a *Running Times* columnist, and an author of training books, wrote workouts for her and taught her the principles upon which she still bases her training. Kruell had another strong coach when she joined a postcollegiate running club.

"I had a lot of guidance in the past [to help me] learn what works for me," she said, which gave her an advantage when it came time to coach herself.

Kastor says Coach Vigil ignited a desire for more knowledge.

"I wasn't always a student of the sport. It wasn't until I graduated from college in Arkansas and had a conversation with Coach Vigil," Kastor said. "He made me a student of the sport. I craved learning more on how to be better physically, how to be better emotionally, mentally."

Grimes praised his coach Jim Hunt at Humboldt State College for teaching, not just directing workouts. "I believe that if you're coached really well and you're taught really well, you can be a better coach of yourself," Grimes said.

Several lifetime competitors dove even deeper into learning when they became coaches themselves. Magill became the head coach of a high school team at age 25. "I read every article that came out, and read every book by every great coach, and made my kids my guinea pigs," he said.

However they started, all consider knowing the sport essential to their ongoing survival as successful runners.

―

WHY IT MATTERS

In an age of personalized online training programs and myriad choices for coaching, does a runner really need to be a student of the sport to continue running through the decades? Perhaps not as much as in the past, but the strategy has several advantages.

One, following a training plan versus self-coaching is a bit like getting directions somewhere versus having a map and knowing how to read it. As long as you never make a wrong turn, you can keep following the directions you were given (turn left at the red barn) and reach your destination. But if you go off course at any point, you're lost. And let's face it, in training, you inevitably go off course at some point. Being a student of the sport and understanding *how* training works puts that map in your hands, along with an ability to read it, so you can find where you are and how to work toward your destination from that location.

Following a training plan versus self-coaching
is a bit like getting directions somewhere
versus having a map and knowing how to read it.

Interactive online coaching is more like a GPS than old-fashioned directions, but it's only as good as the programming behind it and might not match reality on the ground. GPS guidance also doesn't take into account, for example, that you're driving a 1968 Ford pickup that can't handle interstate speeds. Neither can the GPS monitor any changes in capability during the trip.

You yourself are, more often than not, the best judge of where you are and what is the best training for you today. But you need to know where you're going and how you get there in order to give yourself directions.

Solving the Puzzle

Another reason being a student of the sport is important: It gives runners the chance to control the experiment.

"Things that I devote my time to, I'm curious about," said Friend-Uhl as she described talking to coaches, reading, and paying attention. "I'd try out workouts, note what worked and what didn't, get to know my body."

Experimenting isn't just a prerequisite to finding what works and then using that knowledge as you work toward a challenge. The experiment itself can be part of the challenge.

Part of what is exciting about running is that runners must juggle several variables. The challenge isn't only physical but also intellectual, not just about how fast you can run but how you can combine all the elements and adjust each variable to maximize the outcome.

"The more I learned about the human body, the more questions I had about how I could make my body better," Friend-Uhl said. Trying to run your best lets you explore everything from physiology to biomechanics to midsole compounds. It can be an endless source of fascination.

Turns out, this constant study and consequent experimentation is also key for continued motivation as you age. Adding aging to the list of variables that influence performance increases the challenge and interest of the experiment rather than decreasing interest because you're no longer able to run as fast. If the challenge includes the intellectual, introducing a new variable to the puzzle makes it more fun.

Running at 52 isn't the same as running at 28. I'm not simply trying to combine the same elements to repeat what I did before and maybe get a fraction better. I now have new ingredients to include in the mix. Trying to understand and maximize my running today can be as or more fascinating as trying to run my fastest ever with the same parameters. This kind of mastery, an ongoing process with moving targets, is a way that I can be a better runner now than I've ever been, regardless of my finish times.

WHAT SHOULD I DO TODAY?

First, start studying. Information about training is everywhere. Just be careful to assess the source of the information you read, always ask why, and look for how new information fits with what you already know.

Then become your own scientist. Test and verify every piece of advice, both to see if it works and, most importantly, if it works for you. And have fun in the process. It's easy to view experimenting as simply the preparation before you get to doing the real thing. But realize that the experiment *is* the real thing. A finished puzzle is only of interest for a few minutes after it is done; the challenge of putting it together was the point.

You may not always get it right. In fact, that's pretty much assured. But if you view the puzzle as the goal, failures aren't setbacks but stepping-stones.

A finished puzzle is only of interest for a few minutes after it is done; the challenge of putting it together was the point.

Griffin, who has been self-coached all his adult life, mused about things he might have changed in order to have been able to run faster. "If I had it to do all over again knowing what I do now, I would approach it differently," he admitted. He has no regrets, however. He laughed. "I've got to tell you, it was fun!"

KEY 6
STUDENTS OF THE SPORT

- Learn the map: Read all you can, from physiology and coaching philosophies to biomechanics and shoe design.
- Be your own scientist: Experiment, catalog, draw conclusions, and test again.
- Embrace the puzzle: Designing and perfecting a training plan around the unique variables of your dynamic body and mind can be endlessly fascinating.

9

STAYING CONNECTED
NURTURING THE TIES THAT BIND AND MOTIVATE

Watching him go, on and on at that apparently easy, non-flagging
pace, I feel an emotion which I have not felt in a long time:
a certain awe in the presence of ability and determination
far beyond any ambition of my own, a surge of admiration for
the physical beauty of a good athlete in action.

—EDWARD ABBEY, *DOWN THE RIVER*

Marc Bloom had been competing since high school. As an adult, he ran consistently, did some marathons, focused on biking for a while, and at age 59, ran the Fifth Avenue Mile in 5:40.

In his 60s, he began volunteering with local track and cross-country teams and running the workouts with them, trying to hang with whatever kids he could. He discovered two things. One was that he liked this kind of running. Not marathons or half-marathons or accumulating running days or miles, but training for 5Ks the way high school kids do.

"My favorite kind of running and fitness is what high school cross-country runners do, in terms of distance, tempo work, hill work, various calisthenics, competition, and general mindset," he said. "I thrive on that type of program."

The second discovery was that he not only liked it, but it worked. It wasn't long before he was the team coach, and his running was never better.

As a coach, he did workouts with the students a few times a week, which he said got him in the best shape he had been in for years. "It was very motivational and inspirational to try to keep up with them. The fact that I was three times their age didn't matter."

Bloom's coaching is one way that he's created a connection to the sport beyond his own participation. That his own running improved has been a wonderful side benefit. But even more importantly, the connection with other runners provides continuity, motivation, and different perspectives that have helped him maintain his interest and passion for the sport.

Bloom isn't the only runner to discover the motivation and structure of coaching, and how it rejuvenates many masters' running lives.

> *You go to a workout and have a bunch of guys*
> *that want to work hard–you can't help but keep your own running*
> *at a high level when you're surrounded by that in your training.*
> —CRAIG CHRISTIANS

Christians also started volunteering for the local high school team. Soon he was the coach and working out hard with the group.

"I'm not going to go do two hard speed workouts on my own. There's no way," Christians said. "But if I've got a bunch of guys pretty close to ability to me, somewhere in there is a kid you can run with and have them really push you."

Christians said it is a bit like being part of an elite development group like Hansons-Brooks. "You go to a workout and have a bunch of guys that want to work hard—you can't help but keep your own running at a high level when you're surrounded by that in your training," he said. "It's been huge."

KEEPING UP WITH THE PACK

Chris Jones graduated from Bucksport High School in Maine in 1981. A strong runner in cross-country, he didn't run track because it conflicted with baseball, his first love. Today, Jones no longer plays baseball but he is still running and racing well, perennially placing among the top runners for his age group in local races.

Much like Bloom and Christians, Jones credits his continued interest and excellence to coaching. He started coaching track right out of college and took over the cross-country program at his high school alma mater in 1987.

"It's always been easier for me to run, because I'm coaching. It's a lot easier when you know you've got to go out with kids," he said. When the kids go out on the roads or trails, he wants to be there to make sure they are doing the workout and to be available for advice.

When she was in her mid-40s, Maria Spinnler had problems with her back that led her to pull back on her running. But as a coach at the local college, she wanted to at least be able to jog with the team.

"I was not training for anything, just staying in shape so that if I need to run with the kids, I could," Spinnler, now 55, recalled. "If I stop running completely, I feel like I can't go warm up with the girls, talk with them, give them race strategy." It wasn't long until she was healed up enough to start thinking about competing again herself.

Benson, age 75, has been running and coaching for over 50 years. He doesn't race much anymore, but he still trains hard once a year to race the same distance that the high school kids he coaches do in their cross-country meets.

"What I've been doing is try once a year to get in good enough shape to run a 5K," he said. "To remind myself what I'm asking my kids to do—the pure torture and agony of running hard for 3 miles."

This goal gets him out on a rolling dirt training path at least once a week to get in some "really good, hard interval training."

Lindgren has founded several club-level and sub-elite teams and pours himself into coaching, motivating, and creating opportunities for the members to find challenging competition. But he's not willing to just talk about passion and honesty; he puts himself on the line and tries to model what he finds compelling about the sport. "That is my role," he said. "Be that lightning rod for those that want to achieve the most out of themselves."

As a coach myself for the past decade, I recognize all these benefits. In addition, I've found a simple joy and energy by being around young people, which keeps me feeling younger.

Friend-Uhl, also a coach, noted this effect as well. "Like they say, if your dog is getting old and you want to cheer him up, get a puppy," she said. "Running with girls, I feel younger."

She has to work to keep up, especially on short repeats and at the beginning of workouts while she's still warming up. But she finds she can catch them and hold her own as workouts progress. "They force me, in a good way, to ask and expect more of myself, even though I'm older," she said.

WHAT'S YOUR ROLE?

Coaching is one of the most common ways to stay involved in running, but lifetime competitors find many other ways to connect with the sport. Some are race directors, like Jones, who puts on several local races, including the town's signature Tour du Lac 10-miler, now in its 42nd year, or Allen, who created a unique free marathon to bring runners to Millinocket, Maine, as well as directing the Mount Desert Island Marathon and other races in the regions. Several runners serve on regional or national boards of USA Track and Field. Many volunteer at track meets and road races.

Some have found other professions related to running. The options are surprisingly varied: podiatrist (Zenker), director of footwear testing at Nike (Paulk), elite athlete agent (Reilly), race timer (Durden), camp director (Benson), online and club coach (Buciak), broadcaster and public figure (Switzer), fitness trainer (Coates, Friend-Uhl), author, journalist (Bakoulis, Bloom, Chase, Douglas, Magill, Robinson, me). None of these jobs involve running as an actual work task, but they keep us in association with runners, thinking about running, and giving back to running as a sport.

WHY IT MATTERS

Soon after leaving college, Benoit Samuelson coached the women's track team at Boston University. She was still training and racing herself, but she noted the importance of having something besides her own running. "Working with them made me think about something besides myself," she wrote in *Running Tide*. "Self-absorption is a great danger to those who participate in solitary activities like running."

Of all the reasons outside connections are good for us as runners, this might be one of the most important. Thinking about others' running gives us some perspective and emotional space, space we need to be emotionally agile. It's easier to evaluate someone else's running than our own, to assess the relative importance of goals and times, to see the cycles and the circumstances of their training, hopes, successes, and failures. Armed with that perspective, it is easier to recognize when we are getting too emotionally hooked on our own running dramas.

Having connections to the sport also helps a runner ride out the inevitable downtimes that occur in any running life. Part of the reason people fall away from running is simply that they lose contact. They get injured or busy and have to take time off, and soon they don't have anyone or anything that reminds them that the sport is going on.

Coaching, directing a race, timing, volunteering at an event, writing about a race—all these keep you in touch with running and runners. Through these myriad connections, you are reminded of the joy, the pain, the passion, and the satisfaction. Even if you've been hurt or burnt, this has a way of drawing you in again; you want to taste it yourself.

Ikigai

In *The Blue Zones*, a book about societies where people are more likely to live to be 100, Dan Buettner says that one of the keys to this longevity is to have a life purpose. In Okinawa, they call this *ikigai*, which translates to "why I wake up in the morning."

For passionate lifetime runners, running is the *ikigai*. Certainly this gets harder to sustain with age, when more days arise in which you can't run, be it due to injury or just the need for an extra day off. What I heard from lifetime competitors across the board was that while they had not lost any of their passion for training and competing, their other connections with the sport also provided purpose and meaning. Their involvement with the sport acted as another outlet for their passion, sustaining them as they aged and helping remove fear of the future.

Fanelli has coached and mentored young athletes for 20 years, which he finds motivating and satisfying. His focus is on being the role model older runners were for him when he was young. "I perspire to inspire," he said. "It's a prime ambition. Hopefully I'm making a difference in setting an example."

Another deep satisfaction for him comes from seeing others succeed. "Nothing beats helping other athletes get to the next level," he said.

"I know if I stopped running, my running would continue as a coach," Paulk said. "I'm still running now—it's a dual joy. But I know someday, if I cannot run, I can channel my running drive into teaching and mentoring young folks."

Fanelli, Paulk, and many others revealed that their connections to the sport beyond their own running provide a wider, deeper purpose. And rather than distracting them, this wider meaning keeps them interested in running while at the same time removes some of the pressure that might push them over the edge.

WHAT SHOULD I DO TODAY?

You may or may not have the skills and experience to get hired on as a coach for the local track or cross-country team. You can, however, volunteer to help out at the meets. You can also ask if you can run with the kids in practice (being careful to get the blessing of the coach and assure her or him that you won't be giving contradictory advice).

One of the easiest ways to get involved is to volunteer at a local road race or crew or pace an ultrarunner doing a 100-mile race. Find out if your area has a USATF chapter, and help put on the youth meets. Create a website for your local running club. Write a club newsletter or your own blog.

Another way lifetime competitors stay connected to the sport is as avid fans. They watch races on TV and follow top runners. Edward Abbey described the awe and admiration of watching a Hopi youth run a race, "the physical beauty of a good athlete in action." After watching an Olympic Trials marathon or a marathon major, I'm always inspired to lace up my shoes and go for a long run of my own. And in the end, what pro runner Kenenisa Bekele does on the streets of Berlin is no different from what we do on our suburban sidewalks every morning. Take away the clock ticking off sub-5:00 miles, and he's running at the edge of his ability, trying to get the most out of his body, just as we are.

If the difference between your speed and effort and the elites' simply feels too great, then head over to a local college or high school meet.

You'll see the same struggles, the same grit, the same pride all of us feel when we race. Seeing this and the youthful passion on display is a reminder of what it feels like to compete. Don't be surprised if you find you want to feel it yourself.

KEY 7
STAYING CONNECTED

- Be inspired: Running with or simply watching young, enthusiastic runners motivates you to act and feel younger as well.
- Bridge the downtimes: Having a context to be in touch with runners and racing keeps you close to the sport and motivated to return.
- Broaden your purpose: Caring about others provides perspective and meaning apart from your own running.

10

HOPE
THE POWER OF OPTIMISM

I never can be argued into hopelessness.

–HELEN KELLER, "OPTIMISM: AN ESSAY"

In 2002, Mark Buciak of Chicago, then in his early 40s, went in for his annual physical. A veteran of 50 marathons with a PR of 2:30, he expected to breeze through as usual and then celebrate his good health by eating a deep-dish pizza and donating a pint a blood. Instead, he was told that he had a leaky heart valve, a congenital defect that was worsening quickly.

Three and a half years later, the valve had deteriorated so much that a replacement was imperative. The surgery was successful, but with a cow valve grafted into his heart, Buciak was told to keep his pulse under 130.

You might expect this to be the end of the story, at least as far as running goes: Once a runner, Buciak was now just happy to be alive. That's not the end, however. I met Buciak in the lobby of Boston's Copley Square Hotel in 2016, the day before his 37th consecutive Boston Marathon, his 10th consecutive with a cow valve.

He walked the course in 2006 a few weeks after the surgery. Since then, he's been running and racing regularly, aiming simply to do his best with his body today, taking into account the new variable of how much his repaired heart can handle.

You might think this shows how well adapted Buciak was, that he was never obsessed with times or external success and that he always had an easy time simply running to appreciate the moment. That would be wrong too.

After a string of consecutive low-2:30 marathons in the '80s, he got a full-time job, and although he felt he was training as hard, his times fell to the mid-2:40s. He found the slide difficult to come to grips with. "I was the most depressed person in the world," he said.

Today, he laughs at his youthful self and at how foolish it was to lament such good times. What's clear to him now is that everything is relative. Mostly, he is grateful that he never stopped running, not because of disappointing times or because of open-heart surgery.

"[Running] was in my DNA, in my blood. This is what I do," he said.

DIEHARDS

Buciak is clearly an exceptionally driven individual who refuses to let anything stop him. But he's no outlier, I discovered, as stories like his started piling up.

Sperandeo, hit by a drunk driver while on a run, didn't walk for a year, let alone run. But with hope and persistence, he eventually came back, ran a 2:29 marathon at age 40, and still competes at a top level on the track. And if that weren't enough, he also overcame cancer and radiation treatments at 50 and still continues to run and race.

Zenker, a competitive runner since high school, was in his mid-30s when he went to the doctor feeling run down and thinking he had the flu. He found out instead that he had a rare genetic form of type 1 diabetes. During the ensuing weeks, while getting insulin injections and learning what he would need to do to manage his health, he was sure his running was over.

But a few weeks later, he ventured out on a run. Not knowing how his body would respond, he wanted to be prepared. "That first time, running around the block, I had a backpack with enough food and supplies for two weeks!" he recalled.

The run went well, and within three weeks, he was back to running 15-milers and racing 10Ks. In 2009, at age 45, he qualified for and ran Boston. "It's not easy, with diabetes," he said. But he said it is similar to other life pressures: "You either give up or you're still competitive and you work this stuff in and enjoy it."

Ruben, a 2:30 to 2:40 marathoner into his 50s, had a stroke at age 58. At first, he assumed he wouldn't run again. "I was wobbly," he said. "I couldn't walk properly." But after a couple of weeks, his balance improved and he thought, *I should get up every morning and go for a walk like I used to get up and go for a run.* Before long, he wondered what would happen if he tried to run. Eventually, he worked back to basically doing what he did before.

The stroke has slowed him down, but he finds great satisfaction in giving the same kind of effort. "I'm doing the same kind of workouts, similar mileage, same methods; it's just all slower. I'm not up as high— I used to always be in the top 3, now I'm like fifth or sixth."

He's since run three marathons. And furthermore, he's optimistic that he'll improve. He was looking forward to turning 60 at the time I interviewed him. "That might psychologically boost me," he said.

After being diagnosed with Parkinson's disease, Michael Westphal thought his running days were over. Then he discovered that running actually reduced his symptoms, and so he immediately started training for a marathon.

He's fallen to the ground in four of the six marathons he's run since, usually in the final miles as he starts to fatigue and push the edge, but he always gets back up. He's still setting goals, training, and competing well at 60.

Durden keeps training, keeps racing, keeps pushing after two rounds of cancer and treatment. Robinson got a knee replaced in his early 70s and is today gleefully setting age and artificial-knee PRs while chasing down other septuagenarians in races on the East Coast.

THE POWER OF OPTIMISM

What was driving these runners, I wondered. It was crystal clear that they were motivated individuals who didn't accept no for an answer. But was this genetics and upbringing, or was there something to learn here that the rest of us could emulate?

As I pondered this question, I returned to Duckworth's book, *Grit*. The title, of course, describes lifetime competitors well, and I recognized their characteristics throughout the book. But the "aha" moment came in a chapter titled "Hope."

I realized that hope is what these runners all had in common, not a naïve wish that things might be better, but rather, as Duckworth described it, "the expectation that our own efforts can improve the future" and a refusal to quit in response to adversity.

To explain hope, Duckworth pointed to research by Marty Seligman that distinguishes between pessimists and optimists. "Optimists are just as likely to encounter bad events as pessimists," she wrote. "Where they diverge is in their explanations: optimists habitually search for temporary and specific causes of their suffering, whereas pessimists assume permanent or pervasive causes are to blame." Optimists always think things can be overcome.

I once heard Nike's Jeff Johnson talk about recovering from a stroke. When you're in rehab, he said, you can always tell who the athletes are. The athletes have transformed their bodies before, they believe in the rehab work, they apply themselves, and they assume that the setback is temporary, not permanent.

Buciak's story—and Robinson's and Sperandeo's and countless others'—reveals exactly this kind of optimism. Consider Douglas's reaction when he was told after surgery that he would never again run more than 20 miles a week: "What is that based on?" he asked skeptically, and today he's running 60-plus miles without difficulty.

Lifetime competitors, forever navigating from a place of hope, have a hard time accepting permanent diagnoses.

About the time I was reading Duckworth, I traveled to Millinocket, Maine, to run a race and continue my interviews. One evening, sitting around a table with lifetime runners Chris and Margaret Jones and Margaret's sister Pattie Craig, I discovered a missing link in my thinking.

I was pushing Chris, 54, to elaborate on when and how he had adjusted to running slower as he's aged. Ultimately, he concluded that he hadn't yet. Referencing this town's 10-mile race, which he'd once won in 56 minutes, he said, "I've always felt that I can't run it in under 60 anymore because my job won't allow me to [train as much as I need to]. It's a time issue."

Knowing that he's always been able to get faster before, he chooses not to ascribe his current slower speed to anything permanent. "I'm not that fast because I haven't been training as much," he insisted. "I believe I could be. Deep in my mind, I'm thinking, *Maybe it is because I haven't trained enough, that is why I can't keep up.*"

Jones pointed to a competitor of his, Bob, who is nearly 10 years older and who is crushing him in races. "He runs with the college boys," Jones said. "In my mind, I'm thinking, *If I ran with the college boys I could run with him.* He does a lot more miles than me. He runs 50 miles a week. If I get a 40-mile week in, that's a big week."

His optimistic attitude was the same attitude that helped runners overcome adversity such as heart surgery, diabetes, or knee replacement. That kind of hope wasn't limited to the dire cases; rather, it was present in every lifetime competitor. And whether it was true that Jones could get back under 60 minutes for 10 miles, the belief that he might empower him.

"That's what partially keeps me motivated," he said. "Hope."

CHOOSING OPTIMISM

Are hope and optimism simply ingrained characteristics? Is the answer to how to be a lifetime competitor similar to the answer to how to win the Olympics: Choose your parents well?

These questions drove me to dive deeper into Seligman's work, which focuses on what he calls "learned optimism." Seligman believes optimism is a skill that can be learned. While early life experiences can predispose us toward helplessness or optimism, it is possible to undo habits of pessimism, learn to choose optimism, and maintain hope.

Many lifetime competitors learned that they could overcome adversity when they went from "not very good" to "I got a lot better." In this journey, they discovered that genetics weren't destiny and that they could present an alternative explanation for mediocre performance.

They didn't view a lack of initial success as permanent and pervasive (*I'm slow, I'm not an athlete*) but rather specific and temporary (*I haven't trained, I can improve my fitness and speed, I can transform my body*). In the coming years, they learned through overcoming countless injuries and navigating family and career challenges that nothing was career ending. They learned optimism.

After having the meniscus removed from his knee in his late 20s, Griffin was told by his surgeon to stop competitive running, and the doctor warned him that it would lead to arthritis.

"I didn't give it a second thought," Griffin said. "And I'm glad I didn't." He went on to run and compete strongly throughout his 40s. And although he has developed arthritis in his 50s, he has no regrets about the more than 20 years of running he enjoyed after that warning. Today, he still runs, races, and maintains hope.

"Since I developed the arthritis, there's been a lot of starts and stops, but I've still not given up the desire and the attempt to get back to consistent training and compete again," he said.

WHY IT MATTERS

"Optimism is the faith that leads to achievement," Helen Keller once wrote. "Nothing can be done without hope."

Hope keeps runners from falling into despair despite injury, aging, and slowing. It recognizes that the world is malleable, as is the aging process. It gives us a reason to keep training when we're healthy and allows us to believe we can come back when life pushes us down. Hope is a bedrock characteristic of the successful athlete at any age.

"Hundreds of studies show that pessimists give up more easily and get depressed more often," Seligman wrote in *Learned Optimism*. Optimists, in contrast, overcome setbacks, achieve more in every realm, age better, and live longer.

Is there a downside to hope? Can it be viewed as naiveté, leading to foolish risks or expensive quests that have no chance of success? Does learning optimism mean sacrificing realism?

"There is a dangerous optimism of ignorance and indifference," Keller warned. True, but while optimism can foolishly ignore reality, it certainly doesn't have to. The best kind of optimism focuses on the positive and believes in the best outcome while still being based on reality.

The pitfalls of hope can be avoided if you adopt a flexible optimism, one that recognizes real barriers, downsides, and negative emotions, and understands that different settings make optimism more or less useful.

To this end, Seligman views optimism as a tool rather than a personal trait. Just as you might with any tool, you can use Pollyannaish optimism in certain circumstances and healthy, skeptical pessimism in others.

No one denies that aging doesn't affect performance. "Some losses in physical function . . . are intrinsic to age and therefore inevitable," write Robert Kahn and John Rowe in *Successful Aging*, which argues that lifestyle choices are more important than genes. "However, the losses experienced in the course of what we have called 'usual aging' are a combination of the inevitable and the preventable, more often the latter." The challenge is to discern which losses are which. The optimist assumes everything is preventable until proven otherwise.

Hope is a bedrock characteristic
of the successful athlete at any age.

Optimism is a powerful tool wielded frequently by lifetime competitors in circumstances where they chose not to believe setbacks were permanent and instead believed that they could always be better.

WHAT SHOULD I DO TODAY?

If you haven't developed learned optimism, or if you, like me, still find your first reaction to adversity tends to be pessimistic and catastrophic, Seligman has advice and techniques to develop it.

Learning optimism requires first recognizing the voices you hear when you encounter adversity and, when necessary, arguing with the beliefs behind those voices. As an aid to work through how you talk to yourself about problems, Seligman uses the mnemonic ABCDE: Adversity, Beliefs, Consequences, Disputation, Energization.

When you encounter adversity, your beliefs determine the consequences of that adversity. Pessimists tend to apply beliefs that are permanent, pervasive, and personal, for example, "The whole world is falling apart, nothing will ever be the same again, and it is my fault." Optimists, however, believe that most things are temporary and external.

The day after I read Seligman, I was able to apply his framework on a 10-mile run that included a 3.5-mile segment at tempo pace. I've been trying to break 1:30 again in the half-marathon since I turned 50 three years ago. Every time I've tried, I've fallen short, but I've always found a temporary and external reason for not meeting the goal: I was racing at altitude, the course was too hilly, the weather was too hot or cold, or I had a minor injury.

I have not let go of the goal, however, and was thinking about it as I started the tempo portion of the run. Applying the "run by feel" approach I've learned from the likes of Benoit Samuelson and De Reuck, I didn't focus on my Garmin to try to stay at 6:50s but rather settled into what *felt* like tempo effort. I didn't look at my watch at all until it beeped at the 1-mile split. To my dismay, it read 7:12.

My initial thoughts were pessimistic—*I guess I'm too old. I've waited too long. I'll never be able run that fast again.* The consequences of that reaction were immediate: I lost motivation to push through the workout or even to train for the half-marathon at all. I considered cutting the tempo section short and not rescheduling it. Why not just go long and forget about trying to run fast?

Quickly, however, I recognized what I was doing and began to dispute the pessimistic voice with alternative explanations. I hadn't given lunch enough time to settle. I hadn't yet adjusted to the unseasonably warm weather. I was carrying a small backpack. This was only the second real speed work session of the season. I hoped to run the race at sea level, 3,300 feet lower than where I was training. And, most importantly, I can get faster—that's what training has always done and what it can still do, even if I am aging.

The argument energized me to keep pushing along at the same effort, focusing on relaxing and optimizing my form. The next three splits were 7:04, 7:00, and 7:00. Still not the 6:52 I needed, and being realistic, it's likely that I can't run 1:30 today. But I felt far better about the effort, and what's key is that I have hope that, with more training, I still can, and perhaps eventually will, break a 1:30.

Not Just Cheery Thoughts

In my arguments against my negative belief, I used mostly alternative explanations for the slow split. Sometimes, however clear, undisputable facts can overthrow pessimistic beliefs.

Craig, 51, demonstrated this type of reframing. After she turned 45, she kept getting slower and slower. Depressed, she felt the slowing was inevitable, blaming it on aging. Three years later, however, she discovered that she had been suffering from Lyme disease all that time. This radically altered her perspective and renewed her hope.

"Now that I know that's what happened, maybe I can train hard again," she said. "Maybe I can actually do something good again."

Honest Optimism

Learned optimism isn't blind. It attempts to counter knee-jerk pessimistic beliefs with facts and alternative explanations for the adversity you face. As a final option, however, if the facts confirm your negative belief and you can't find any alternative explanations, Seligman recommends focusing instead on the implications of the belief.

A pessimistic view goes immediately to the most dire outcome: Everything is permanently and completely buggered. The optimistic argument "decatastrophizes" the situation. It says things like, "So what, is that result so bad? Is everything broken or only specific parts? Are there alternative outcomes that could be positive?"

Applying this process to my training for a sub-1:30 half, yes I *am* getting older (fact); my tempo pace is slower than I used to be able to run in a full marathon (fact); and at some point, I will not be fast enough to run a 1:30 half even when running as hard as I can in perfect conditions (no alternative explanations). My pessimistic reaction is to believe I'm broken, that it's no longer worth training hard, that there's no reason to set a goal, and there's hardly reason to run except for maybe getting out to jog once in a while so I don't get too fat.

Accepting the facts, I can still argue their implications. So what if I'm not as fast as I used to be? I'm still fit from years of running, and in relatively good shape for a 52-year-old. And what is special about a 1:30 half-marathon? In the end, it is something that I myself have tagged as the dividing line between "good" and "slow"—but is it really? Not many years ago, I considered a "good" half to be sub-1:20.

Sure, it sucks to be aging and getting slower—I can mourn that—but that isn't cause to give up competitive running. I still enjoy racing and training for a race. If I can't get excited about setting a slower goal time for myself, why not set another goal that has what Benoit Samuelson calls a "story"? Maybe "sub-5:30 at 53 for the mile." Or, I could try to run faster than my first marathon, 37 years later. Or qualify for Boston again.

And, focusing on today, this workout, I can enjoy simply running hard, holding my foot to the pedal at that red line threshold for 25 minutes.

This provides that same feeling of being a fine-tuned machine now, running at a 7-minute pace, as it did in 1996 at a 5:50 pace.

> *Learned optimism isn't blind.*
> *It attempts to counter knee-jerk pessimistic beliefs with facts*
> *and alternative explanations for the adversity you face.*

Addressing negative facts with optimism is the process of adapting discussed in Chapters 6 and 7. It means not giving in and giving up but instead adjusting goals and expectations to appropriate levels, ones that are enough out of reach that you must work to meet them, but not so far out of reach that they overwhelm. It also means acknowledging the emotions that come along with these adjustments, and then unhooking from them so you can move forward.

This process, which turns the focus on the many ways running can still be appreciated, also brings us to the diverse facets and multiple levels of love that lifetime competitors have for the sport, which is, appropriately, the topic of the final chapter.

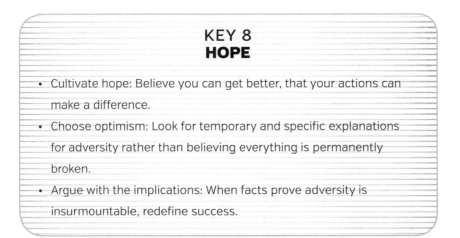

KEY 8
HOPE

- Cultivate hope: Believe you can get better, that your actions can make a difference.
- Choose optimism: Look for temporary and specific explanations for adversity rather than believing everything is permanently broken.
- Argue with the implications: When facts prove adversity is insurmountable, redefine success.

11

LOVE
IT MAKES THE WORLD GO 'ROUND

Love . . . is a constant challenge; it is not a resting place,
but moving, growing, working together.

–ERICH FROMM, *THE ART OF LOVING*

One winter evening during his junior year in high school, Benson
went out for a run in Stevens Point, Wisconsin. He had been a runner for
nearly two years and had started to fall in love. This evening, however,
was special. The temperature was about 30 degrees Fahrenheit, cool,
crisp, and invigorating, and it had started snowing softly. It was pitch
dark, except for the light thrown by street lamps.

A girl Benson liked had just agreed to go on a date with him, and he
was thinking about her as he ran down the middle of the street, moving
out of the darkness into the streetlight and back into the darkness, fluffy
flakes sparkling as they fell through the air and caressed his cheeks. It
was magic.

"I remember the unbelievably wonderful feeling to be out running
like that," Benson said. "That was the moment when I was really hooked."

It's a love story, the kind they make movies about: the heart-stopping
moment when you catch eyes across a crowded room, the first kiss.

Not all of them are as poetic as Benson's, but every lifetime runner told some version of falling in love and staying in love for a lifetime. Of all the keys to a lifetime of running, the greatest of these is love.

GROWN-UP LOVE

Love may start with a magical moment, but to sustain a relationship for a lifetime, it must grow and deepen. This is the love I heard described by lifetime competitors.

This is a mature love, not a high school crush or the giddy passion of newlyweds. This is the love of a long-married couple. They've been side by side through good times and bad, through ups and downs. They know each other's weaknesses and faults. They've disappointed each other at times. At others, they've wowed, exceeding all expectations.

They've been so frustrated that they've separated, maybe more than once, yet they've always chosen to come back together. They still expect passion, but not every day—they can also be happy walking quietly together, holding hands. They can no longer remember or imagine a life apart.

I could fill this chapter with quotes from lifetime competitors about how wonderful and essential running is in their lives. Indeed, this book is rich with them:

"When I was hurt and couldn't run, the colors just weren't as bright," said Friend-Uhl. "Running is this huge part of my life. It's always been there. My best friend, if you want to call it that."

"I just loved to run," said Coates. "Nothing was going to get in the way: I was going to run. I still do. Nothing is going to keep me from continuing to run."

"Nothing can replace running," Pillin said. "There's nothing like it. I don't know what it is."

It truly is a love affair.

SPLIT PERSONALITY

Is it racing that lifetime competitors love so much? Or is it the joy of running itself?

Almost universally, I found lifetime competitors loved both the act of running and the thrill of competing. Indeed, many said these were so intertwined, it wasn't an either/or question.

"Both running and racing are important," said Dunham. "The running isn't really a means to an end for racing, but I love the competition as much as I love the training for it. I'd say it is even."

The degree of passion for each side differed in each runner and changed over time. But even if these two loves appear at times contradictory, loving both sides of the running life seems to be an important key to longevity, perhaps because together they help to keep runners engaged through the years.

In his book *After the Last PR*, Griffin wrote colorfully about this split personality.

> *Two runners live inside me. The first one . . . is a fierce competitor, daring and tenacious. He lives for brief, glorious moments, like the instant when a competitor's footfalls begin to fade behind him. His expectations are unquenchable. Seldom is he satisfied, even when he wins . . . .*

The second runner can go for miles without thinking once about speed. He thrives on the motion, the simple rhythm that makes him feel at home. He seeks peace, not recognition.

When I asked Griffin about the two runners inside him, he said, "I need them both." Many others agreed.

I've often noted these two runners in me, personified by the two lead characters in the classic movie *Chariots of Fire*. I harbor both the fire of

Abrahams, who is going to "take them on, one by one, and run them off their feet," and the mellow peace of Liddell, loping over the hills, who says that when he runs, he feels God's pleasure. These two runners inside of me trade the lead back and forth, sometimes the competitor motivates the runner; sometimes the runner sustains the competitor.

A lifetime competitor's love of running includes pleasures unique to each of these internal runners.

PUSHING THE EDGE

When it comes to racing, many lifetime competitors enjoy pushing their limits, getting outside of their comfort zones. And while many runners are willing to endure the pain of racing in order to accomplish a goal, lifetime competitors clearly enjoy the effort for its own sake.

"I like competition," said Maria Spinnler. "I like the feeling of going out there and giving all I have. Then I can feel good about myself."

I've heard similar language before. In *The End of History and the Last Man*, Francis Fukuyama wrote about those who "will deliberately seek discomfort and sacrifice, because the pain will be the only way they have of proving definitively that they can think well of themselves, that they remain human beings."

Fukuyama wrote this in the context of needing opportunities for struggle in today's culture of comfort and ease. He referenced the philosopher Hegel, who believed one of the characteristics that makes mankind unique is the ability to overcome our desire for self-preservation and fight to the death over nothing more than a symbolic idea. Animals will fight to the death in self-defense or to preserve their homes, but only humans will risk our lives solely for the sake of risking them, to prove to ourselves and others that we can and will. Whenever we choose a painful and difficult path in pursuit of an intangible goal, we affirm our humanity.

Applying this to racing, feeling good about ourselves stems from the opportunity the effort gives us to show that we are in control, that we choose and act. It reminds us that we're not drifting along, taking the path of least resistance to simply survive and be comfortable, slaves to basic desires and pleasures. The fact that we will push beyond the body's distress signals for no good reason but ego is the whole point. It is a way to prove to ourselves that we have a will, that we're fully human.

It's healthy to want this pain, and racing is a good, safe way to feel it and affirm that we are still the directors of our lives. What is more, the feeling doesn't change with age, as it isn't dependent on speed or skill; the effort is the key.

"I still have not found anything as satisfying personally as going out and trying to get the best of myself in something as simple as a race," said Griffin.

A common stereotype is that older people no longer need to prove anything and that they can go gentle into that good night. Runners I talked to disagree. "Competitiveness never stops," said Zenker. Kathrine Switzer agrees. "You think that I could get to a stage where I didn't have to keep proving things to myself, but I'm not sure life ever answers that," she said.

Lifetime competitors are like Boston Red Sox slugger David Ortiz, who told *Sports Illustrated* during his final year in the majors, "The reality is a lot of us give up on chasing things as we get older . . . In my case, man, I chase things still."

STILL A CONTENDER

We don't need to race to feel good about ourselves, of course. But for many, there is a deep satisfaction that comes from head-to-head competition, competing not just against our lower instincts but also against the will of others. Many lifetime competitors thrive on this competition.

Esty-Kendall described a half-marathon he ran last fall. Esty-Kendall is in his late 60s and has mellowed considerably from his younger, competitive self. Going into this race, he had the idea that he'd just run it to finish and see where his fitness was. With a couple miles to go, however, he discovered that he was running next to a guy in his age group. "I put him away, I hate to say it," Esty-Kendall told me. He decided when to surge, put in his move, and the other guy didn't follow.

In this he found the same feeling he had felt as a high school runner 50 years ago, he said, and it brought him that same satisfaction. It's nice, he added, to be reminded that he's still got that.

Gordon Bakoulis, one of the top masters in the country in 2002–2003, still runs daily at age 56 but no longer specifically trains for races. "The older you get, just showing up and doing your thing counts as racing," she said, laughing. But she does like to take her fitness for a spin about once a month, and she says her competitive juices come alive whenever she shows up at a race.

"Going to a race and putting on a number gets me jazzed up," she said. "I like that feeling of running fast, running hard, and chasing it."

There's the personal desire to test limits, but Bakoulis also gets a buzz from head-to-head battles. "I like competing with people," she said. "Even if it is someone you don't know and will never see again. This person and I are running neck and neck—let's try as hard as we can and see how it goes."

For her, it isn't about winning but rather about inspiring stronger effort. "As soon as you cross the finish line, it doesn't matter who crossed first," she said. "Whatever compels you to take it to your highest level, you can at that moment."

The thrill of head-to-head competition never ages. As long as you have the ability to move, this love never has to fade.

MAKING SOMETHING HAPPEN

Beyond race day itself, I found another aspect of competition beloved by lifetime runners. A race introduces a goal and a deadline for running, a benchmark to work toward. Setting and achieving goals provides satisfaction and meaning. This process is central to what keeps runners motivated and compelled by the sport.

"If I have a race in four months, it makes those four months so much more interesting," said Friend-Uhl. "Being able to work toward something, challenge yourself, see how close you can get, that's what makes me feel alive. That's what makes me want to wake up tomorrow and do it all over again."

The steady progression of more challenging goals and increasing skills is a constant, compelling obsession—until it isn't. At some point, the graph peaks and starts down. Up to this point, the line of progress had always trended upward; you put in the work and you got better. How can you set a goal when you know that no matter how much work you put in, you're ultimately going to get slower?

To keep this love intact requires strategies discussed in previous chapters, such as scaling goals appropriately, trampling on the past, doing regular resets. The aging decline needs to be included in the list of given variables. You can still find satisfaction in hitting a target, even if the target is to slow the decline.

Although they lamented not being able to get better and talked about the difficulty of finding meaningful goals after the last PR, lifetime competitors still embraced having goals and having races on their schedule. Even if they didn't meet a goal, they found having one valuable because as their competitive side chased success, it brought along that "other runner" inside them, the one who revels in the process and the simple act of running.

THE GLORY OF THE EFFORT

In his book *Flow,* Csikszentmihalyi commented on a curious relationship between goals and effort. "Goals justify the effort they demand at the outset," he wrote. "But later, it is the effort that justifies the goal."

On one side, this cyclical process makes accomplishing goals more special. The actual accomplishment, no matter how limited or arbitrary, carries the weight of all the work that went into it.

Paulk talked about this in relation to his 800m racing. He said oftentimes people question why he would fly all the way to, say, Spain for a 2-minute race. He explained that it was far more than that. "You don't understand," he'd respond. "That 2 minutes is not 2 minutes, it's 52 weeks of training and long runs and intervals and the shitty weather and the sleet storm that I had to do that workout in."

Every runner who has done a marathon knows that a marathon isn't 26.2 miles and a few hours long. It is *hundreds* of miles, put in over multiple months—all those miles you need to transform yourself into the runner who can handle the distance and the pace. Those miles, and that concomitant transformation, are what gives it meaning and are part of why we love it.

BEACONS

On the other side of the Csikszentmihalyi equation is the fact that the goal first justifies the effort. It justifies the effort and compels it if the goal is ever to be reached. So even runners whose main goal is to stay fit enough to enjoy running and keep doing it for life love competing because the goal helps them maintain the effort.

"Competing is a funny thing," said Magill. "I don't actually care whether I win or lose or even do that well in a race once the race is over." What matters to Magill is the daily training—long runs with clubmates, running fast on workout days, seeing what his body can do.

"Races give you something to wrap that training around," Magill said. "They give me a reason to run. If I'm not getting ready to race, I'm going to find it very hard to convince myself that I should go out and do long hill repeats or 200s on a track."

The funny thing is that he enjoys all of those types of runs, and he enjoys being as fit as he can be, which requires doing a full range of workouts. But he finds he needs the race to provide the deadline and motivation.

"If I wrap it around a race, I give myself a focal point. It's kind of like I'm steering for a beacon," he said. "So races serve more as beacons for me than they do as individual tests that I need to pass for my ego or motivation."

"Races keep you honest," offered De Reuck. "It is more exciting to train toward something than to just train." She agrees that the real reward is to get out and run every day, to be fit enough to enjoy running long and well. But when she doesn't have a race on the calendar, De Reuck ends up skipping one day, then another, and soon finds she hasn't trained much in several weeks.

A race helps her find the time and gets her out the door. "It gives you that extra drive rather than, 'I can skip this day.'" De Reuck said. "It gives you extra motivation."

ABOVE ALL, THE RUN

As much as they enjoyed competition, however, I found that every life-time runner also loved the run for its own sake. It is not a means to the end; it has its own meaning. It's hard for competitors to separate running from racing, but when forced to look at it, they concur that the running comes out on top.

Benoit Samuelson said she's always had a goal and she loves racing even now. But when asked if she runs only to race, she didn't have to think long. "I guess if somebody told me you'd never race again, I'd get over it pretty fast," she said. "If someone told me you could never run again, I wouldn't get over that very fast."

"I'm just glad I can get out the door, get my run in. It feels great," Rodgers said. "I still like to race, but that becomes the ultimate satisfaction with your running."

Lifetime competitors listed the myriad reasons you often hear about why it is great to be a runner. You might call them side effects: mental and physical health, social connections, a unique and enjoyable means of transportation, the post-run euphoria.

When they talked about what lies at the core of their love for running, however, they tended to come back to a feeling of being competent, alive, and skilled, a feeling of catching the wave and being carried along, a feeling of flow. They talk about heading out and settling in to an effortless long run.

"What is really fun now," Esty-Kendall said, "is just being able to run and feel like I'm running easily and smoothly, and the distance doesn't matter."

"There's that euphoric feeling," said Margaret Jones. "If I can run 10 miles, run around the lake, I feel like a queen for the day,"

"The ultimate is to get on a country road and keep going. And go as far as I feel like running that day," said Erickson.

Again and again, lifetime competitors rhapsodized about this state— this ability to go out and immerse in a run—as the very heart of their love affair with running. It's not training for something else. It needs no justification or reward. It is the reason.

Lydiard referred to it as a "tireless state." Runners achieve this state when they have "sufficient stamina to maintain their natural speed over whatever distance they are running." When achieved, it produces the characteristics of flow: time slows or stops, you feel in control even as you lose the burden of self-consciousness, you become the run.

It's not as mystical as it sounds. It's simply the result of skill meeting an appropriate challenge. To achieve this state requires consistent miles, a variety of speed work, and, for some, hours of supplementary training. Races help you stay focused and on track, and they have their own pleasures and benefits, to be sure. But this ability to run, free and effortlessly, is what people come back to in the end and what makes it all worthwhile.

COMFORTABLE IN LOVE

"If you come to terms with what your body can do so you feel comfortable running at that pace, it doesn't matter how fast you are going," Esty-Kendall said.

Every year, Esty-Kendall runs a relay called the Katahdin 100 in northern Maine. One year his segment included the infamous Abol hill, about a mile long with several steep pitches, which he encountered during the middle of the night.

Because it was pitch dark and he was running alone, he simply settled in to the effort that felt right. He wasn't trying to keep up with anyone. Since he couldn't see the top of the hill, he didn't anticipate the future relief and push harder until he got there. He wasn't trying to maintain a particular pace.

It wasn't until he approached the relay exchange at the top and heard someone mention the hill that he realized he was even on one. "*I just ran Abol hill?*" he recalled thinking. "*I didn't realize it.*" In the dark, without the context telling him it was hard or he was slow, he ran the pace that felt right for his body.

This is what he's doing now, in every mile he runs. "I'm right here now," Esty-Kendall said. "Whatever the pace is. Feel the pace, rather than the distance or time. That's what I'm trying to do now." It is the key to his continuing love of running, 52 years after he first ran around a track.

In *The Art of Loving*, psychologist Erich Fromm described this mental state as concentration and claimed it a prerequisite for love. "To be concentrated means to live fully in the present, in the here and now, and not to think of the next thing to be done while I am doing something right now," he wrote.

> *Turn off the other voices and measurements and memories,*
> *and tune in to how the run feels now, noticing and appreciating*
> *being alive, active, and meeting the challenge of the moment.*

We need to turn off the other voices and measurements and memories, and tune in to how the run feels now, noticing and appreciating being alive, active, and meeting the challenge of the moment. That's the key to settling in to a tireless, timeless state. Learning this ability to concentrate on now is the sum of all the rest of the book, and the final result. When we can run without doubt or stress, unconcerned about how we compare—to others, to our previous selves, to expectations—the run can go on forever, the love never fails.

=

WHY IT MATTERS

It's safe to say no one becomes a lifetime competitor without love. I'm willing to bet that there are no miserable old runners who took up the vow, gutting it out for 50 years, all the while grumbling that they've always hated it but it's good for them. That said, this doesn't mean they love every run or every aspect of running. Like any relationship, it's complicated and multifaceted. But they all love doing it for its own sake.

Quite simply, running is too hard to do as a means to another end. No amount of winning, weight loss, Strava kudos, or Facebook likes can get you out day in, day out, for weeks and months and years if you have to grit out the actual activity. If you don't love it, you're not going to be able to continue very long. And you probably shouldn't.

When Kruell hears people say, "I should run," she says, "No, you shouldn't. If you don't like it, don't do it." She makes a great point. Find something you do love. The world is a big, diverse place. The answer that is right for me doesn't have to be right for you.

Continuing to run through the years isn't hard for those who love it. They don't see it as discipline but as a treat, a friend, an escape, an indulgence, a pleasure.

Said Kruell, "If there is something about it that you really love, that thing gives back to you. Once you find that joy, it is really easy to go forward, really easy to keep going."

WHAT SHOULD I DO TODAY?

If you do want to run for life but are having some trouble with the love part, don't despair. Burfoot said, "I think you can learn to love the sport if you don't feel it originally, which many don't."

By exploring and experimenting,
you can find the part of the sport that trips your trigger.

Burfoot pointed to learning to appreciate being outdoors (see the sidebar "Get Outside") as a way in for many runners. But there are other ways. By exploring and experimenting, you can find the part of the sport that trips your trigger. You might find your joy in the social aspect of running and racing, or in being alone with nature, or in seeing places you haven't been before, or in the feeling of being part of a team.

It doesn't have to be one thing. In fact, appreciating multiple parts of the sport helps carry you when you tire of one aspect and the passion wanes. At times, you may enjoy an audacious challenge, at others, a quiet morning jog. You may find later in life that you learn to relish short all-out efforts when once you avoided them because you felt you lacked leg speed. "Love is a many splendored thing," as the saying goes.

All these things, however, are parts of the sport, not the act itself. How do you build love for running itself? How do you find that easy, smooth, tireless state that lifetime competitors describe as the essence?

GET OUTSIDE

One benefit of running that was frequently mentioned by lifetime competitors is that it gets you outside. Not just out the door, but actively immersed in the environment and, ideally, out in nature.

"I like to be outside and moving and breathing. For me, that is such a blessing, such an outlet for my day," said Kruell.

Burfoot talked about feeling lucky that from the beginning, he was "running through apple orchards and not doing intervals on the track" and he learned to love the way running allowed him to interact with the environment.

Bakoulis cited this as a major motivation for her daily runs in New York City. "Every day, I look around at nature," she said. "The trees, the changing seasons, the sun, the moon, the wind, the river." She says being a runner gives her a chance to appreciate the beauty around her that she otherwise might miss.

"If I had to run on the road all the time, I might not do it," Robinson admitted. "I want to get out into whatever the weather is, the environment is. I want the experience."

Considerable research backs Robinson up on this, showing that people who exercise in nature are more likely to continue, as well as get more out of the exercise. A 2011 systematic review of related studies concluded, "Compared with exercising indoors, exercising in natural environments was associated with greater feelings of revitalization and positive engagement, decreases in tension, confusion, anger, and depression, and increased energy." They also found that "participants reported greater enjoyment and satisfaction with outdoor activity and declared a greater intent to repeat the activity at a later date."

Jim Costor, a lifetime competitor and an oncologist, pointed me to several studies that show how simply getting outdoors improves every aspect of exercise, and indeed life. He feels it as well, noting that "outdoor running has a calming, uplifting, clarifying effect on me."

In addition to the physical, cognitive, and emotional benefits, Costor sees a spiritual one as well. "I suspect that one reason time outdoors helps broaden our perspectives, minimizes the microstressors of daily life, and restores a proper hierarchy of priorities is because in the great outdoors we are small, we realize as the days and seasons pass that everything we see has an expiration date, thus time is precious," Costor said. "And these notions have a humbling effect, which tends to be calming and stabilizing."

Find Your Flow

To find flow, the first step is to realize that love isn't an emotion. It isn't falling in love as much as it is the *practice* of love that Fromm wrote about in *The Art of Loving*: "Love isn't something natural. Rather it requires discipline, concentration, patience, faith, and the overcoming of narcissism. It isn't a feeling, it is a practice."

Running love requires much the same. When people don't enjoy the act of running, it's usually because either they haven't developed enough skill to meet its challenge or they set the challenge too high or too low.

When you start out, running itself is hard, especially if you expect to go fast. Lowering expectations from the beginning helps, but you still need work to build enough skill to where it becomes interesting. In flow theory, low skill meeting low challenge results in apathy, even if they match each other.

Initially, you have to put in the consistent work with discipline, concentrating patiently with hope that you will get better. Once you start to get better, then the joy starts. As we've seen, you don't have to be empirically "good at it" to enjoy the benefits.

"Olympians do not have an exclusive gift in finding enjoyment in pushing performance beyond existing boundaries," Csikszentmihalyi wrote in *Flow*. "Every person, no matter how unfit he or she is, can rise a little higher, go a little faster, and grow a little stronger. The joy of surpassing the limits of the body is open to all."

Once enough skill is reached to run comfortably, the key is then scaling the challenge to match that skill. Sometimes people don't set the bar high enough and slip into boredom. Others push too hard and are always slightly overwhelmed and looking forward to when they can stop.

It sounds like it should be easy to match our running with our skill level, but we have many forces pushing us to exceed expectations, from our own ego to comparisons with others, our overall sense of hurry, and a need to get done quickly. And eventually, we're pushed beyond our skill by what we've learned and come to expect we "should" be able to do but no longer can as we age.

Harmonious Passion

Finding this balance includes managing the power of the running identity and the obsessive tendencies of such a passionate love. Those who have successfully navigated through the decades have developed what psychologists call a "harmonious passion." Those with such a love "are not compelled to do the activity but rather they freely choose to do so. With this type of passion, the activity occupies a significant but not overpowering space in the person's identity and is in harmony with other aspects of the person's life," Robert Vallerand wrote in a 2003 journal article, "Les Passions de l'Âme."

In contrast, those with an obsessive passion feel they must run because running is so integral to their identity that they have to live up to expectations, real or perceived. Obsessive passion tends to interfere with enjoyment of the sport and the runner's ability to focus and perform at his or her best. "I get to run today" turns into "I have to run today"—and I have to run at a certain level.

A 2015 study of participants in the World Masters Athletics Championships by Bradley Young and colleagues shows that masters competitors tend to have harmonious passion more often than their younger counterparts. They have worked out how to persist in the sport without the conflicts of obsessive involvement. Their running isn't a caustic, overwhelming love where they ditch their jobs and relationships so that they can run more—or wish they could. That kind of imbalance leads to either resenting the other demands or resenting the sport.

Harmonious passion leads to the balance that many successful masters talk about. They love running but recognize the constraints of other parts of their lives and factor these in as variables they have to weigh when they assess their success. Like their natural leg speed or their age, they accept the time, energy, and resources they have available for the sport. Honestly assessing that they are giving all they can at this stage in their lives, they deem it still worth doing.

"You have to be confident and comfortable with a level of discipline and sacrifice," said Fanelli. "Being that I was never good enough to make an Olympic team, I have not compromised the rest of my lifestyle."

Lifetime competitors expressed this healthy perspective on running's importance: very high, essential, but one of many priorities. Indeed, they didn't get here without such a perspective, as it allows them to continue to choose and love running at whatever level they can do it today.

KEY 9
LOVE

- Embrace your split personality: The competitor and the runner within you complement and carry each other through a running life.
- Love the run: Learn to appreciate the act of running by concentrating on the now.
- Strike a balance: Match the challenges you face to your skill level to experience joy and satisfaction.
- Find harmony: Make peace with the level of commitment your life allows.

AFTERWORD
WHY BE A LIFETIME COMPETITOR

If you can fill the unforgiving minute
With sixty seconds' worth of distance run,
Yours is the Earth and everything that's in it . . .

−RUDYARD KIPLING, "IF"

Most of you who are buying and reading a book on how to be a lifetime competitor probably have a desire to be one or perhaps already are. But the questions are worth exploring: Why should any of us want to be lifetime competitors? Is there value in continuing to train and race year after year? Is it worth the time and effort, or does it make our later years a disappointing shadow of our former running selves as our abilities decline?

Note that these questions differ from whether it is worth running for life. Given the many undeniable physical and psychological benefits that running provides, that seems to be a given—yes, it is worthwhile to run for as long as possible, and then to at least keep walking.

But is it valuable to keep pushing yourself, to keep competing?

As I wrap up my time with the subjects who provided the background of this book—51 runners I've lived with for months—and pore over our conversations until they are mostly memorized, I have to say yes.

Each lifelong competitor I talked with was notably enthusiastic, passionate, mindful, self-aware, hopeful, and happy. They were young and vivacious, regardless of age.

I believe being lifetime competitors has helped them become remarkable people.

Chapter 11 talked about how racing reaffirms our ability to choose actions and directions other than the path of least resistance. This process is not only satisfying but also character building. When we put ourselves in a competitive situation and force the choice between taking it easy or pushing, between giving in or showing up, those who regularly choose the harder path develop a strong sense of personal willpower and integrity.

In *The Willpower Instinct*, Stanford psychologist Kelly McGonigal describes how willpower can fatigue as well as get stronger through training. Studies have revealed that subjects who perform self-control exercises show significant improvement in their capacity for willpower. "It was as if they had strengthened their self-control muscle," McGonigal wrote.

Lifetime runners recognize and appreciate this. "I realize now that so many disciplines that I use in my day-to-day life were crafted through running," said Griffin.

Fanelli listed several aspects honed in running that he says undoubtedly helped him be a success in business: focus, concentration, discipline, visualization, the ability to set goals and to see them through in spite of obstacles. "What you do in the sport carries over into the rest of your lifestyle and accomplishments elsewhere," he said.

"Running has taught me to push my limits and my boundaries and learn how to grow spiritually and mentally," said Kastor. "It is my avenue for growth. I'll never retire from it. All this mental and physical and emotional strength I practiced to be a better runner I can continue to practice to be a better person through running."

ENGAGED AND FORWARD-LOOKING

Another notable trait shared by lifetime competitors is that they don't spend much time in the past. They're too busy planning and dreaming about the future. The very process of scheduling a race makes you look forward; it assumes that you will continue training from now to that date.

Racing provides accountability and ensures you stay engaged. You can't just think about running or do a little bit and hope it is enough. You can't fake a race. Whether or not you've done the work is going to show when you toe the line.

Scheduling a race is also an act of hope. You dare to believe you can get better, that you can have success in this endeavor. And, unlike many areas of life, you have considerable control over that success, which is empowering.

"I didn't ever intend to be a lifelong runner," said Magill. "But one of the reasons I couldn't put it away is that every time something got a little tough in life—I didn't have the job I wanted, or didn't get the girl I wanted, or something didn't go right—I knew I could run. I could put on my shoes, I could start doing some distance, I could throw in some workouts, and I could improve. I could go from not being in great shape to being in really good shape. And I could have success at that."

REAL AND HONEST

Carl Jung said in an interview on his 85th birthday, "An ever-deepening self-knowledge is, I'm afraid, indispensable for the continuation of real life in old age, no matter how unpopular self-knowledge may be."

Running has the ability to provide this self-knowledge, which allows for the continuation of real, honest living. Lifetime competitors appreciate this, even when what it reveals can be painful. "It keeps you honest," Fanelli said about racing. "There's always the guys out there whose focus is on where they used to be. It's nice to recognize where you've been, but you have to be here now. And have some sense of where you're going forward."

The clear, unarguable facts of racing that we loved in our youth can still provide a measure of where we are and anchor us in today's reality, if we have the courage to face and accept it. "That's the black-and-white beauty of the sport: its measurability," Fanelli says.

Lindgren echoed this praise for the uncompromising truth of the race. "It's an opportunity for honesty. Nothing is as cleansing. It's all based on where am I today."

To get the most out of running, Lindgren said, "You have to accept it in its most stark and brutal honesty. The more honest you are, the more you'll get out of running and life. Running always gives back more than you put into it, and the more you put into it, the more you get out of it."

Among many other good reasons to continue, not only as a runner but also as a competitor, this one stands out: because you will get more out if you put more in. "The quality of experience tends to improve in proportion to the effort invested in it," Csikszentmihalyi said. The higher the skill, the greater the challenge, the more joy and satisfaction.

Maximizing our potential is one of our basic needs. Psychologist Abraham Maslow defined this desire for self-actualization as "the desire to become more and more what one is, to become everything that one is capable of becoming." Declining physical ability need not thwart this desire. Maslow included the desire to know and understand as an aspect of self-actualization, and each day provides a new context in which to become more fully what we are.

JOY ABOVE ALL

Some readers may have come to this book for hard-core training advice. Indeed, were this a seminar, I can imagine getting to this point and after talking about acceptance and flow, honesty and joy, having someone raise their hand and ask, "So, do I have to run intervals to win races in my 50s?"

There is enough of that type of information in this book to go forward confidently. But I don't apologize for focusing on learning to run freely, with joy. More than any training detail or trick to make yourself stay disciplined, finding enjoyment in running itself is the key to staying in the sport and staying competitive.

Kastor credited her longevity to being "positive and optimistic." She said she gets lots of sleep and pays attention to nutrition, but more importantly, she said, "I really live my days in a joyful way, I don't have a lot of resistance or angst to live with, and my body has held up well."

FILLING THE MINUTES

"These are our few live seasons," Annie Dillard wrote in *Pilgrim at Tinker Creek*. "Let us live them as purely as we can, in the present."

Everyone over 30 knows that time slips away faster and faster every year. Lifetime competitors want to live those minutes, and running well is one way to live them purely and in the present.

Whatever our pace, whatever our age, we want to fill the unforgiving minute with 60 seconds' worth of distance run. For, while we still can, ours is the world and everything that's in it.

CONTRIBUTING RUNNERS

Allen, Gary

Age: 60, running since 1972

In his 45 years of running, Allen has finished 101 marathons, 68 of them in under 3 hours, with a 2:39 PR. He is one of 39 known runners to have completed a marathon faster than 3:00 in every decade from the 1970s to the 2010s. A race director and fund-raiser/social advocate through running, Allen is looking forward to continuing to compete in the 60+ age groups.

Bailey, David

Age: 54, running since 1979

Bailey primarily focuses on the 800 m and 1500 m. His best marks, 1:51.0 and 3:45.3, respectively, were set in college in the late '80s. His masters 800 m PR is 1:59.7, and he ran 2:08.85 at age 51 at the 2014 USATF Masters Outdoor Track Championship, earning him second in the 50–54 division.

Bakoulis, Gordon

Age: 56, running since 1978

Bakoulis has a marathon best of 2:33:01 and qualified for the US Olympic Trials for marathon five times. She won the masters division of the 2001 New York City Marathon in 2:41:39 and was named the New York Road Runners' Female Runner of the Decade in 2010. A former editor of

Running Times, Bakoulis is a coach, author, and journalist with the New York Road Runners.

Benoit Samuelson, Joan
Age: 60, running since 1972

At age 21, Benoit Samuelson won the 1979 Boston Marathon in a course record 2:35:15. She set the world record of 2:22:43 in 1983 and won the first women's Olympic marathon in 1984. She qualified for seven Olympic Trials for marathon and is the only woman to appear on a list of those who have run a sub-3:00 marathon in five different decades. Her best, 2:21:21, was set in 1985, and she ran a 2:52:10 at the 2014 Boston Marathon, at age 56.

Benson, Roy
Age: 75, running since 1956

Benson started as a middle-distance runner and achieved best times of 1:53.4 for 880 yards and 4:19.8 for the mile. Going longer, Benson set masters PRs of 4:52 for the mile, 36:06 for 10K, and 3:09:05 for the marathon. He has been involved in the sport for 55 years as a coach, writer, lecturer, and camp director.

Bloom, Marc
Age: 70, running since 1958

Bloom began running in junior high track and started writing about the sport as a high school cross-country runner. He set most of his PRs around age 40, including a 17:45 5K and 37:12 for the 10K, and has won several New Jersey masters age-group titles in track and cross-country. He ran 5:02 in a road mile at 40 and a 6:06 mile at 69. He often trains with the high school kids he coaches and continues to try to break 20 minutes in the 5K—but lately is happy with sub-21.

Buciak, Mark
Age: 57, running since 1974

Buciak ran his first marathon at age 15 in 3:11:13. He ran his best time, 2:30:25, at the 1983 Boston Marathon. Buciak has now run 61 marathons and 38 consecutive Bostons, the last 11 with a replacement heart valve. He shares the wisdom he's learned over 140,000-plus lifetime miles while coaching his The Road to Boston training program and as a writer and public speaker.

Burfoot, Amby
Age: 71, running since 1962

Coached by 1957 Boston Marathon winner John J. Kelley, Burfoot won the Connecticut state 2 mile his senior year in high school and the 1968 Boston Marathon as a senior in college. His ran his marathon PR of 2:14:29 at Fukuoka later in 1968. He has run the Manchester Road Race for 55 consecutive years. At 60, Burfoot posted a 1:27:40 for the half-marathon, and at 70, he finished the 2017 Boston in 4:18, becoming the fifth known runner to have completed a marathon in each of seven decades of life.

Chase, Adam
Age: 51, running since 1978

Chase, although a soccer player in high school, ran a marathon his senior year. He competed in cross-country his senior year in college and expanded to triathlons and ultras. He has run a 2:39 marathon and a 3:32 50K, and set several course records in trail ultras in the Rocky Mountains in the '90s and early 2000s. Chase was an international competitor in the short-lived adventure racing circuit and now runs 50- to 60-mile weeks and spends an hour or more a day on gym work to be fit enough to run whatever he wants.

Christians, Craig
Age: 56, running since 1972

Christians got into the sport in junior high track and has run consistently during the 45 years since. At his best, he set PRs of 15:28 for 5K and 1:11:39 for the half-marathon. In his 40s, he posted 15:59 and 1:15:43, respectively, at those distances. Last year, at age 55, he ran an 18:36 5K and a 1:23:22 half-marathon, and put in 2,200 miles, his second highest annual total ever.

Coates, Budd
Age: 60, running since 1972

During his lifetime of running, Coates has qualified for four Olympic Trials for marathon. He set his marathon PR of 2:13:02 at the 1983 Boston, and he's on the list of those who have run a sub-3:00 marathon in each of the past five decades, the latest a 2:47 run in 2011 at age 54. A coach and author, at age 56, he ran a 1:20:18 at the hilly Runner's World Half Marathon in Pennsylvania.

Coster, James
Age: 56, running since 1972

Coster, primarily a middle-distance runner, has competed in the sport since elementary school track. Except for a brief hiatus during medical school, when he ran minimally, he has run and raced consistently for over 40 years, from the NCAA finals in college to the occasional major meet as a master. On a good day, he can still run his age in the 400 m. An oncologist at the University of Kansas Cancer Center, Coster is a student of exercise physiology and masters training.

Craig (Clapper), Pattie
Age: 51, running since 1977

Craig started racing at age 11, accompanying her parents and older siblings to road races and meets. In high school, she bettered numerous records set by her older sister Margaret, including running 5:20 for the mile and 11:26.4 for the 2 mile. After college, she took some time away from the sport, but returned in her 30s. As a master, she's run 21:41 for 5K, 43:26 for 10K, and a 3:33 marathon. When newly 50, Craig placed sixth woman overall in a mountain challenge race.

Cucuzzella, Mark
Age: 51, running since 1980

Cucuzzella began running as a preteen, covering 10 or more miles barefoot on New Jersey beaches. He had a successful high school and college career and, postcollegiately, ran a 1:08 half-marathon and 2:24 marathon. Injuries led to a major foot surgery at age 34, following which Cucuzzella relearned to run barefoot, reviving his competitive career. An advocate of natural running shoes and technique, Cucuzzella has now run over 100 marathons and ultras, and has finished a marathon in under 3 hours for 30 consecutive years, posting a 2:56 at the 2017 Boston Marathon.

De Reuck, Colleen
Age: 53, running since 1980

De Reuck competed in four Olympic Games, from 1992 to 2004. She has set two world records—51:16 for 10 miles and 1:05:11 for 20K—placed second at the 2002 World Cross Country Championships, and won the 1996 Berlin Marathon with her PR of 2:26:35. As a master, she set 10 American records, including a 2:30:51 marathon at age 46. She won her age group at the Ironman World Championship in 2011, and in 2016, at age 52, she ran the iconic Comrades ultra in her native South Africa for the first time, placing seventh overall.

Douglas, Scott
Age: 53, running since 1979

Douglas started in high school cross-country and quickly learned to love miles on the road. After moderate success in school, he put in solid training in his 20s and posted PRs of 30:48 for 10K, 51:01 for 10 miles, and a 1:08:40 half-marathon. As a writer and editor for running publications, he has run over 110,000 miles and continues to run doubles and do a variety of workouts, though he races sparingly.

Dunham, Dave
Age: 53, running since 1978

Dunham has been a top competitor since high school and college, where he ran 4:10 for the mile and a 14:08 5K. He has a 2:19 marathon best and placed second at the World Mountain Running Championships in 1993. He's run more than 135,000 lifetime miles, and while he mostly races trails and mountains, in his 40s he posted a 1:15 half-marathon and he's run 1:19 for the distance in his 50s.

Durden, Amie
Age: 61, running since 1980

Durden began competing in road races in Atlanta during the first running boom. Before long she was running marathons, with a 3:27:46 PR in 1987. She set her masters PR, 3:50, at age 51, which converts to 3:10:40 when age graded. At 60, she ran 4:22:37, which also converts to a 3:10:40, displaying her remarkable consistency. She's run every day since October 30, 2003, and has completed over 125 marathons, with at least one in every state and the District of Columbia.

Durden, Benji
Age: 66, running since 1964

Durden started running in junior high school track. In high school, he ran a mile in 4:36, then lowered that time to 4:15 in college with minimal training. It wasn't until after college that he started training regularly and competing well, posting a 2:36 for his first marathon. He eventually ran a 2:09 marathon best and made the 1980 Olympic marathon team. Lately, Durden has been collecting marathons: He has completed a marathon in all 50 states plus DC, all in under 4 hours, and has run over 125 lifetime marathons.

Emery, Robin
Age: 70, running since 1967

Emery started running before women were supposed to sweat, and she won nearly every race she entered for years. She won the Portland Boys Club 5-Miler 13 times, with a PR of 29:06, and the Bangor Labor Day 5-Mile Road Race 14 times, the latest at age 51. Some of her best races came in her 40s, including a 17:45 5K and a masters division victory at the 1991 Tufts 10K in Boston. When she was inducted into the Maine Running Hall of Fame in 1990, they estimated that she had won more than 255 races. Last year, at age 69, she ran 1,300 miles and competed in 43 races.

Erickson, Roxi
Age: 54, running since 1976

Erickson ran her first marathon when she was 13, on the rural roads of her Nebraska home. She competed in high school but had the most success in the marathon in her 30s, when she was able to crank out times between 2:45 and 3:00 seemingly at will. She won the Lincoln Marathon for 10 consecutive years, from 1994 to 2003, and set the course record of

2:42.20 in 1996. She ran her PR of 2:39:25 at Grandma's Marathon in 1996. She continues to love running daily and regularly places in the masters division of local road races.

Esty-Kendall, Judd
Age: 67, running since 1965

Esty-Kendall chose the mile in high school track, thinking he could avoid doing much work, and quickly discovered he had some talent for going long. He continued running on his own through college and started road racing in graduate school. It wasn't until his 40s, however, that he ran his best times, with a 2:43 marathon best. He won a half-marathon in 1:18 at age 52. Today, he's more relaxed in his racing, unless there's someone near him in his age group.

Fanelli, Mike
Age: 61, running since 1970

Fanelli started running in high school track, where he ran a moderate 4:41 mile and 10:07 2 mile, but he improved dramatically in college, achieving a 14:44 5000 m. He completed his first marathon as a 16-year-old in 3:36 and eight years later lowered that to 2:25. Fanelli has coached for more than 20 years, including the elite Impala Racing Team and three USA national teams. He broke 5 minutes for the mile at age 50 and recently surpassed 107,000 lifetime miles while continuing to compete in middle-distance track and chase the All-American standards.

Friend-Uhl, Sonja
Age: 46, running since 1981

Friend-Uhl has been at the front of the pack at races from the mile to the marathon (2:49 PR) for three decades, from winning the 800 m and cross-country state titles in high school through setting the world record in the women's masters indoor mile (4:44.81) and the American record in the outdoor 1500 m (4:16.99). A fitness professional, running coach, and mother of two daughters, Friend-Uhl now competes in masters cross, track, and on the road. In early 2017, she ran a 1:22 half-marathon and broke Benoit Samuelson's indoor 3000 m American record, running 9:53.

Griffin, Dave
Age: 56, running since 1976

Griffin started running in high school after being cut from the freshman basketball team because he was too small. He ran the JFK 50 Mile while still in high school and started road racing seriously in his 20s, posting 1:12:24 half-marathon and 32:10 10K bests. After meniscus surgery and a stress fracture, he raced little in his 30s. He came back in his 40s and set masters bests that included a 17:16 5K and 1:23:25 half-marathon. Today, though slowed by knee arthritis caused by the removed meniscus, Griffin continues to love running and racing while coaching the runners in his Flying Feet Running Program. He is the author of two books, *After the Last PR* and *In the Distance*.

Grimes, Dan
Age: 58, running since 1972

Grimes started in junior high and ran through college at Humboldt State University. After graduation, he earned enough winnings from road races to run full time for a while. He qualified for three Olympic Trials and represented the United States in the marathon at the 1987 World Championships in Rome. His best times include 13:51 for the 5K and a 2:13:12 marathon. Today, he runs in the mountains and, although he seldom races, stays in enviable shape.

Jones, Chris
Age: 54, running since 1976

Jones ran his first road race at age 13. A varsity high school runner, he posted best times of 4:29 for the mile and 10:10 for the 2 mile. In college, he ran 25:25 on a 5-mile cross-country course. Post-college, he ran a 44:48 in the 8.2-mile Great Aloha Run in 1986 and won the hilly Tour du Lac 10-miler in 56:01 in 1987. At age 41, he ran his half-marathon best of 1:24:10. Jones has coached cross-country for 29 years, directs local races, and continues to place well in his competitive age group.

Jones (Clapper), Margaret
Age: 54, running since 1977

A standout high school runner, Margaret Jones posted school records at nearly every distance, including 5:25 for the mile and 21:34 for the 5K. She returned to the sport as a late-20s college student, was the Little East champion in cross-country in 1992, and ran times such as 10:39 for the 3000 m, a school record. Jones continues to compete as a master, with highlights of 20:18 for the 5K and a 75:01 10 mile.

Kartalia, Steve
Age: 51, running since 1979

A high school state champion in cross-country and the 2 mile, in college Kartalia ran a school record of 29:38 for the 10K at Wake Forest University. After struggling with injuries, he, along with his coach, Doug Renner, found a formula for steady progress post-collegiately, and Kartalia qualified for the 1992 Olympic Trials in the 10,000 m with a 28:32. In 1996, he qualified for the marathon trials, running a 2:18. As a master, he's enjoyed competing on a cross-country team at USATF club nationals and continues to race on the roads, posting times as fast as a 1:16:23 half-marathon in September 2016, at age 51.

Kastor (Drossin), Deena
Age: 44, running since 1984

After starting running at age 11, Kastor won three California state cross-country titles in high school and was a four-time SEC champion at the University of Arkansas. She placed third in the 2004 Olympic marathon in Athens and holds six American road records, including the marathon mark of 2:19:36, set in London in 2006. She's qualified for five consecutive Olympic Trials and made four Olympic teams. Since turning 40, Kastor has set numerous US and world masters marks, including the masters world half-marathon record of 1:09:36 and the American masters marathon record of 2:27:47. She's also explored new challenges, such as competing in the Beat the Sun relay race around Mount Blanc in the French Alps.

Kruell, Kelly
Age: 58, running since 1975

Kruell qualified for state in high school cross-country and track, and set school records in the mile and 2 mile (11:23—still standing). At Cornell, she was cross-country captain for two years and set the school record in the 10,000 m. After college, she ran PRs that included 16:48 for 5K, a 1:19:01 half-marathon, and 2:52 for the marathon. As a master, she's run 18:33 5K and 1:24:18 half, but she mostly competes in cross-country. She has run in 15 consecutive USATF Cross Country Club Championships, and 12 USATF Cross Country Championships, where she won the 55–59 division in 2016.

Lang, Kent
Age: 55, running since 1976

Lang started running in high school after discovering he wasn't going to grow into a basketball player. He continued to develop and run faster every year up until his 30s, eventually running a 2:23 marathon in 1990. A consistent high-mileage runner, he's racked up over 117,000 lifetime miles, has run every day since February 28, 2006, and still runs 5Ks in the 18-minute range.

Lindgren, Will
Age: 59, running since 1972

After starting running in high school, Lindgren maintained fitness in his 20s, then got seriously into the sport in his 30s, setting PRs that included 33:55 for 10K and a 2:46:56 marathon. In 2008, he won the USATF 50–54 title at the 25K road championship in 1:53:25. Lindgren has been actively involved in USATF leadership, and he has founded and coached several running clubs and elite teams.

Magill, Pete
Age: 56, running since 1975

Magill had an on-again, off-again running career from high school through his late-30s, running strong enough to be a two-time California Junior College Cross-Country All-American and set a PR of 5:09 for 2K. In his 40s, he started to excel, setting times like 3:56.42 for the 1500 m at age 41, a 14:34 5K at 46, and the world's best time at 5K for age 49 at 14:45. A coach and author of running books and articles, Magill is a five-time USA Masters Cross-Country Runner of the Year, the fastest American distance runner over age 50 in the 5K (15:02) and 10K (31:11), and holds multiple American and world age-group records.

Mirth, John
Age: 55, running since 1975

Starting in eighth-grade track, Mirth ran a 9:33 2 mile by his senior year in high school. He clocked 30:06 for the 10K in college and kept running, qualifying for the Olympic Trials three times and running a 2:19 marathon best in 1986. He's won at least one race a year every year since he was a freshman in high school. Mirth runs over 2,000 miles per year, usually far more than that, putting in more than 4,000 miles during several years. At 42, Mirth placed fourth in the masters division of the 2004 Boston Marathon and, at 50, was the age-graded champion at the 2013 USATF Masters Cross Country Championships, running 27:13 for an 89.09 age-graded percentage.

Paulk, Kevin
Age: 57, running since 1973

Paulk first broke 5 minutes for the mile 43 years ago as a high school sophomore, and he ran a 4:30 at age 16. He went on to run a 3:56 1500 m and 14:45 5000 m in college. After years of road racing, including a 2:28 marathon, Paulk returned to the track as a master. He ran 1:58 for the 800 m at age 43 and won the World Masters Championship title at that distance at age 45, in 2006. He has seven individual national titles in the 800 m and 1500 m spanning 12 years, and continues to chase it, running a 5:10 mile in early 2017.

Pillin, Phil
Age: 55, running since 1975

Pillin started running in seventh-grade track, where he says he finished dead last in every race. Through high school and college, running at Bowling Green State University, he was dedicated and enthusiastic but failed to make the varsity squad. He ran his first marathon in the fall of his senior year in college, a 2:36 in Philadelphia, and lowered that to 2:32 the next year. He's averaged over 10 miles a day for 40 years, with a lifetime total of more than 135,000 miles. Pillin is an official for cross-country and track, a race director, and a leader in his local USATF association. In 2016, a year after being diagnosed with prostate cancer, Pillin ran all but three days, totaling 2,796 miles.

Reilly, Brendan
Age: 58, running since 1977

After starting running his senior year in high school to get an easy letter, Reilly got hooked on the sport. He has run 30:21 for the 10k and 67:20 for the half-marathon, and he passed 100,000 lifetime miles in September 2015. An agent for elite runners, Reilly keeps up with them on their easy days and still regularly puts in 40 to 45 miles per week.

Ringlein, Ann
Age: 60, running since 1973

Ringlein started running in high school, when the 800 m was the only option available for women. She found she liked to go long, however, and started running 4 to 5 miles around the track on her own. As an adult, she got into road races, eventually posting PRs of 34:00 for the 10K and a 2:47 marathon. A coach, shoe store manager, race director, and running club officer, Ringlein has continued competing into the masters ranks, running a 37:44 10K at age 44, a half-marathon in 1:25 at 48, and a 19:26 5K at 52.

Robinson, Roger
Age: 78, running since 1952

Robinson started running on a school cross-country club in his native England. By 1966, as a PhD student, Robinson qualified for the national team going to the World Cross Country Championships. After moving to New Zealand and excelling on the road and grass there, Robinson competed as part of his new country's national cross-country team in 1977, at age 37. Robinson won the World Masters 10K Road Championships and the New York City Marathon masters title in 1980, and he set the masters records at the 1981 Vancouver Marathon (2:18:45), at age 41, and the 1984 Boston Marathon (2:20:15), at age 44. At 50, he won world cross-country and road titles and set the age-group record at New York (2:28:01) and in many road races. A knee injury took him out of racing in his 60s, but after a replacement surgery, Robinson again chased competitors and times in his mid-70s, with over-75 PRs such as 5K in 22:17, 10K in 47:30, and half-marathon in 1:46:55. He is undefeated at over-75, including in several American road championships.

Rodgers, Bill
Age: 69, running since 1963

After moderate success in high school and college, Rodgers fell away from the sport briefly, then came back with a vengeance. He famously won the 1975 Boston Marathon in an American record of 2:09:55 and went on to win both Boston and New York four times each. He was the bronze medalist at the 1975 World Cross Country Championships and set a 25K world record of 1:14:12 in 1979. Throughout his 40s, Rodgers set numerous masters records, including 29:48 for the 10K and a half-marathon in 1:08:05 at age 45. Rodgers has continued to race up to the present, still competing and placing in his age group at distances up to the half-marathon.

Ruben, Alan
Age: 60, running since 1985

Except for occasional school cross-country days in his native England, Ruben didn't start running until he was 28 years old, when he trained for and ran the Paris Marathon. He finished in 3:09 and considered it a one-time thing. He's now run 29 consecutive New York City Marathons, with 25 of them under 3:00 and 15 consecutive years under 2:40. He ran his PR of 2:29:54 in the 1998 Boston Marathon at the age of 41. After a mild stroke in 2015 nearly took running away, he recovered to run the 2016 New York City Marathon in 3:12. Ruben is the president of the Central Park Track Club in New York.

Sperandeo, Leonard
Age: 57, running since 1975

Sperandeo has been racing on the track since high school and returned to middle distance as a masters athlete. His bests include a 4:06 mile and a 14:23 5K. On the roads, he posted a 29:19 10K and ran 2:29 in the marathon at age 40. That year, he won the 2001 USATF Masters Championship mile with a 4:21.57. A longtime college and club coach, he has continued to compete over the years despite being hit by a car on a run and enduring a bout with cancer. He recently ran a 5K in 17:49.

Spinnler, Maria
Age: 55, running since 1975

As a high school senior, Spinnler won the Ohio state 800 m title in 2:15.4. At Eastern Kentucky University, she ran bests of 4:51.17 for the mile and 10:41.3 for the 2 mile. From 1985 to 1995, she competed professionally for Reebok, qualified for the 1988 Olympic Trials at 10,000 m with a 33:51.94, and placed fifth at the 1993 USATF nationals in Eugene at 5000 m. After taking second in the 1995 Marine Corps Marathon in 2:52:18, she took time off to have children. Returning to the track, she posted a 4:56.6 indoor mile at age 38. As a master, she's run 17:51 for 5K and 36:52 for 10K. She coaches high school and junior college track, and ran her first ultra in the fall of 2016, completing the JFK 50 Mile in 11:18:39 at age 54.

Spinnler, Mike
Age: 59, running since 1971

Spinnler's first race was the JFK 50 Mile, at 12 years old. He competed in high school and college, with a 14:19.6 indoor 3-mile best, and won the JFK in 1982, at age 24, in 5:53, a course record that would stand until 1994. Postcollegiately, he ran 52:24.8 for 10 miles, a 2:28:18 marathon, and

3:16:50 for 50K. Spinnler has coached high school and college athletes since 1983 and served on the coaching staff for nine US national teams. He continued competing until Achilles surgeries forced him to stop in 2005, when he turned his full attention to coaching.

Stirrat, Reno
Age: 63, running since 1969

Stirrat began running as a sophomore in high school, after everyone else on the football team got bigger but he didn't. He was good enough to garner a scholarship for college, where he ran 14:19 for the 5000 m and a 29:42 best for the 10,000 m. But the marathon is where he has most excelled, setting a 2:19:17 best in the 1979 Rocket City Marathon and a 2:25:17 at age 40. He's the only known person to have run under 2:45 in each of the last five decades. Named the USATF's 55–59 Master of the Year in 2010, Stirrat won the 55–59 age division at the 2010 Boston Marathon in 2:42:27. In 2015, he won the 60–64 age group at the USATF Masters Cross Country Championships. Stirrat has run over 160,000 lifetime miles.

Switzer, Kathrine
Age: 70, running since 1959

Switzer started running in eighth grade to get in shape for field hockey. She continued through high school and college, with infrequent opportunities to compete, and famously ran the 1967 Boston Marathon as K. V. Switzer, the first woman to officially register for and complete the race. She won the 1974 New York City Marathon in 3:07:29 and posted her best time, 2:51:37, at Boston the next spring, the sixth-fastest women's marathon in the world at the time. Switzer has been a highly visible spokesperson for women's running as the creator and director of the Avon International Running Circuit, broadcaster, author, public speaker, and now board chair of the 261 Fearless women's empowerment organization. In April 2017, she completed the Boston Marathon 50 years after her debut, running 4:44:31 in her 40th lifetime marathon.

Swope, Tim
Age: 53, running since 1978

Swope ran in high school and college, achieving times of 14:19 for the 5K and a 4:04 mile. He was the 1984 NAIA Region 7 Cross-Country Champion, posting 28:35 for a 5.85-mile course. After college, he barely ran in his 20s, jumping in a road race here and there. Then, after attempting a marathon without training at age 34, he walked away entirely for nearly two decades. Coming back at age 48, he's training and racing again and has run a 5:16.68 mile at age 50 and a 1:23:11 half-marathon at 51. He was the 2015 New Jersey masters 800 m champion, running 2:11.

Westphal, Michael
Age: 60, running since 1972

Westphal was a strong runner on the cross-country and track teams at Mount Desert Island High School and the University of Maine, where he ran a 4:19 mile. In his 20s and 30s, he ran at the front of road races in Maine, winning the Paul Bunyan Marathon in a PR 2:29:32 in 1980. In his 40s, Westphal, busy raising kids and managing his carpentry business, ran sporadically. In 2006, at age 49, he was diagnosed with Parkinson's disease and thought his running was over, but three years later discovered that training helped reduce his symptoms. He started training seriously again in 2014, has since run six marathons with a 3:32 best, and has no plans to slow down at 60.

Westphal, Rolf
Age: 53, running since 1978

A runner since high school cross-country and track, Westphal ran a 2:54 marathon at age 17 and set his PR of 2:39 eight years later at the 1989 New York City Marathon. He's run a sub-3:00 marathon in every decade from his teens to his 40s. Westphal posted a 36:03 10K at age 42 and a 1:22:38 half-marathon at 51. He's continuing strong into his 50s, and a recent 10-miler in 1:04:44 makes him believe he can go sub-3:00 in this decade as well.

Zenker, Chris
Age: 53, running since 1975

Zenker started running as an expat middle-schooler in Singapore. In high school, he made it to state with a 1:58 800 m and ran his first marathon at age 17, finishing in 3:23. He continued through college, running track and cross-country for the University of Cincinnati with PRs of 24:45 for 8K and 2:29 for 1000 m. In his mid-30s, Zenker discovered he had a rare genetic form of type 1 diabetes but didn't let that stop him from running, still breaking 33 minutes for the 10K. He qualified for and ran three Boston Marathons in his 40s and a 1:21 half-marathon at age 47. Now in his 50s, his quest is to break 40 minutes in 10K for the fifth consecutive decade. He won his age group at the 2017 Azalea 10K with a 40:51.

BIBLIOGRAPHY

Baltes, P., and M. Baltes. *Successful Aging: Perspectives from the Behavioral Sciences.* Cambridge, UK: Cambridge University Press, 1993.

Benoit, J., with S. Baker. *Running Tide.* New York: Alfred A. Knopf, 1987.

Benyo, R. *Running Past 50.* Champaign, IL: Human Kinetics, 1998.

Bortz, W., and R. Stickrod. *The Roadmap to 100: The Breakthrough Science of Living a Long and Healthy Life.* Basingstoke, UK: Palgrave Macmillan, 2011.

Buettner, D. *The Blue Zones: 9 Lessons for Living Longer from the People Who've Lived the Longest.* Washington, DC: National Geographic Society, 2012.

Campbell, J., ed. *The Portable Jung.* London: Penguin Books, 1971.

Coates, B., and Kowalchik, C. *Running on Air: The Revolutionary Way to Run Better by Breathing Smarter.* New York: Rodale, 2013.

Csikszentmihalyi, M. *Flow: The Psychology of Optimal Experience.* New York: Harper Perennial, 2008.

David, S. *Emotional Agility: Get Unstuck, Embrace Change, and Thrive in Work and Life.* New York: Penguin Random House, 2016.

Douglas, S. "Ed Whitlock and the Age of Simplicity: The Masters Great Achieves Excellence by Focusing on the Essentials." Runnersworld.com, February 16, 2010. http://www.runnersworld.com/masters/ed-whitlock-and-the-age-of-simplicity.

Drew, M., and C. Purdam. "Time to Bin the Term 'Overuse' Injury: Is 'Training Load Error' a More Accurate Term?" *British Journal of Sports Medicine* 50, no. 22 (November 2016): 1423–1424. doi: 10.1136/bjsports-2015-095543.

Duckworth, A. *Grit: The Power of Passion and Perseverance.* New York: Simon and Schuster, 2016.

Duhigg, C. *The Power of Habit: Why We Do What We Do in Life and Business.* New York: Random House, 2014.

Dweck, C. *Mindset: The New Psychology of Success.* New York: Ballantine Books, 2008.

Erikson, E. *Identity and the Life Cycle.* New York: W. W. Norton, 1980.

Fink, D., and M. Fink. *IronFit's Marathons After 40: Smarter Training for the Ageless Athlete.* Guilford, CT: Globe Pequot, 2017.

Fitzgerald, M. *80/20 Running: Run Stronger and Race Faster by Training Slower.* New York: Penguin Group, 2014.

———. *Run: The Mind-Body Method of Running by Feel.* Boulder, CO: VeloPress, 2010.

Friel, J. *Fast After 50: How to Race Strong for the Rest of Your Life.* Boulder, CO: VeloPress, 2015.

Fromm, E. *The Art of Loving.* New York: Bantam Books, 1963.

Fukuyama, F. *The End of History and the Last Man.* New York: Avon Books, 1992.

Gabbett, T. "The Training—Injury Prevention Paradox: Should Athletes Be Training Smarter and Harder?" *British Journal of Sports Medicine* 50 (2016): 273–280. doi:10.1136/bjsports-2015-095788.

Gabbett, T., et al. "If Overuse Injury Is a 'Training Load Error,' Should Undertraining Be Viewed the Same Way?" *British Journal of Sports Medicine* 50, no. 17 (September 2016): 1017–1018. doi: 10.1136/bjsports-2016-096308.

Gambetta, V. *Athletic Development: The Art and Science of Functional Sports Conditioning.* Champaign, IL: Human Kinetics, 2006.

GfK. *Physical Concerns Around Aging: GfK Survey Among 22,000 Internet Users (Ages 15+) in 17 Countries.* Nuremberg, Germany: GfK, 2016. https://www.gfk.com /fileadmin/user_upload/country_one_pager/NL/documents/Global-GfK-survey_ Physical-concerns-around-aging_2016.pdf.

Griffin, D. *After the Last PR: The Virtues of Living a Runner's Life.* Westminster, MD: Flying Feet Running Programs, 2010.

Hudson, B. *Coach Hudson's Little Black Book, Redux.* Boulder, CO: Horsecow Publishing, 2016.

Hulin, B., et al. "Low Chronic Workload and the Acute Chronic Workload Ratio Are More Predictive of Injury Than Between-Match Recovery Time: A Two-Season Prospective Cohort Study in Elite Rugby League Players." *British Journal of Sports Medicine* 50, no. 16 (August 2016): 1008–1012. doi: 10.1136/bjsports-2015-095364.

Hutchinson, A. "Change Up Your Running Routine: Tweaking Your Schedule Magically Produces Fast Results." Runnersworld.com, January 23, 2014. http://www.runners world.com/race-training/change-up-your-running-routine.

Jacobs, M., et al. "Going Outdoors Daily Predicts Long-Term Functional and Health Benefits Among Ambulatory Older People." *Journal of Aging and Health* 20, no. 3 (April 2008): 259–272. doi: 10.1177/0898264308315427.

Jones, A. *Age Grading Running Races.* http://www.runscore.com/Alan/AgeGrade.html.

Kahn, R., and J. Rowe. *Successful Aging.* New York: Dell Publishing, 1999.

Keller, H. *Optimism: An Essay.* New York: Thomas Y. Crowell Company, 1903.

Kiely, J. "Periodization Paradigms in the 21st Century: Evidence-Led or Tradition-Driven?" *International Journal of Sports Physiology and Performance* 7, no. 3 (September 2012): 242–250.

Lally, P., et al. "How Are Habits Formed: Modeling Habit Formation in the Real World." *European Journal of Social Psychology* 40, no. 6 (October 2010): 998–1009. doi: 10.1002/ejsp.674.

Magill, P. *25 Keys to Running a Faster 5K.* South Pasadena, CA: Pete Magill, 2017.

Maisoux, L. "Can Parallel Use of Different Running Shoes Decrease Running-Related Injury Risk?" *Scandinavian Journal of Medicine and Science in Sports* 25, no. 1 (February 2015): 110–115. doi: 10.1111/sms.12154.

Maslow, A. *A Theory of Human Motivation.* Mansfield Centre, CT: Martino Publishing, 2013.

McGonigal, K. *The Willpower Instinct.* New York: Avery, 2012.

McGrath, D. *50 Athletes over 50: Teach Us to Live a Strong, Healthy Life.* Dener: Wise Media Group, 2010.

McMillan, G. *You (Only Faster): Training Plans to Help You Train Smarter and Run Faster.* Flagstaff, AZ: Greg McMillan, 2013.

Meardon, S., et al. "Running Injury and Stride Time Variability over a Prolonged Run." *Gait and Posture* 33, no. 1 (October 2010): 36–40.

Muraven, M., et al. "Longitudinal Improvement of Self-Regulation Through Practice: Building Self-Control Strength Through Repeated Exercise." *The Journal of Social Psychology* 139, no. 4 (1999): 446–447.

Noakes, T. *Lore of Running.* 4th ed. Cape Town: Oxford University Press Southern Africa, 2001.

Pink, D. *Drive: The Surprising Truth About What Motivates Us.* New York: Riverhead Books, 2009.

Rauh, M. "Summer Training Factors and Risk of Musculoskeletal Injury Among High School Cross-Country Runners." *Journal of Orthopaedic and Sports Physical Therapy* 44, no. 10 (October 2014): 793–804. doi: 10.2519/jospt.2014.5378.

Seligman, M. *Learned Optimism: How to Change Your Mind and Your Life.* New York: Vintage Books, 1990.

Svendsen, I., et al. "Training-Related and Competition-Related Risk Factors for Respiratory Tract and Gastrointestinal Infections in Elite Cross-Country Skiers." *British Journal of Sports Medicine* 50, no. 13 (July 2016): 809–815. doi: 10.1136/bjsports-2015-095398.

Vallerand, R., et al. "Les Passions de l'Âme: On Obsessive and Harmonious Passion." *Journal of Personality and Social Psychology* 85, no. 4 (2003): 756–767.

Watson, A., et al. "Subjective Well-Being and Training Load Predict In-Season Injury and Illness Risk in Female Youth Soccer Players." *British Journal of Sports Medicine* 51, no. 3 (February 2017): 194–199. doi: 10.1136/bjsports-2016-097326.

Whitlock, E. *The Training of Ed Whitlock.* https://canute1.wordpress.com/2014/08/02/the-training-of-ed-whitlock/.

Young, B., et al. "Examining Relationships Between Passion Types, Conflict, and Negative Outcomes in Masters Athletes." *International Journal of Sport and Exercise Psychology* 13, no. 2 (2015): 132–149.

Young, B., et al. "Explaining Performance in Elite Middle-Aged Runners: Contributions from Age and from Ongoing and Past Training Factors." *Journal of Sport and Exercise Psychology* 30, no. 6 (December 2008): 737–754. doi: 10.1123/jsep.30.6.737.

Young, G. "The Art of Living." (Interview with Carl Jung) *Sunday Times* (London), July 17, 1960.

INDEX

ACKNOWLEDGMENTS

Writing this book gave me the opportunity to spend hours with dozens of amazing runners who shared with me their passion and joie de vivre. I never felt like a journalist conducting interviews; each conversation quickly became like a discussion between comfortable training partners on a long run. I am grateful for the time each spent, their honesty, and the trust, respect, and warmth they showed toward me.

I would never have written this book had I not myself fallen in love with the sport. The credit for starting me on this path goes to the late Anne Norton, cross-country coach of Bucksport High School, Maine, who taught me to love running itself, inspired me to dream big, and showed me how to put in the quiet and humble work necessary to get there. I was also blessed with the models of Charlie and Leona Clapper, parents of my teammates (and occasionally my surrogate parents on race entry forms) who demonstrated the joy of running and racing at any age such that the idea of competing for life was inherent in my view of running from the start. Their son, Gerry, was my first running hero and inspired me to excellence while running alongside me and treating me as an equal, even though my skills were far inferior. The list of others who inspired me, helped me, and ran alongside me throughout the years is far too long to include, but I'm grateful for all of you.

I'd like to thank Casey Blaine, my editor at VeloPress, for believing in the concept of this book and for her insightful advice and respectful suggestions throughout the process—from deciding on the book's format to her final, careful editing. She gently guided the book's evolution from a collection of conversations to an organized, readable exploration of lifetime running principles while keeping my prose succinct and focused. Copy editor Faith Marcovecchio patiently pored over every comma and citation, ensuring consistency throughout the book in content and style.

Finally, I want to thank my wife, Tracy, for her invaluable assistance in getting this book written. From the beginning, Tracy listened to and interacted with my ideas, and encouraged me always to keep the writing honest, practical, and accessible to all runners. She is the one to thank if you've found value in this work despite never considering yourself a competitor. She also supported and sustained me through the long hours of interviewing and writing, and patiently waited for me to emerge from the months when all my available mind space was devoted to distilling and describing these principles.

ABOUT THE AUTHOR

Jonathan Beverly fell in love with running as an unathletic but persistent high school freshman in the fall of 1977. He's never stopped. His passion for the sport compelled him to write about it while pursuing a career directing international exchange programs. He began publishing articles in a variety of magazines, which eventually led to his becoming editor in chief of *Running Times* magazine from 2000 to 2015. During those years, he wrote a popular monthly editor's note, more than 35 feature stories and dozens of training articles, athlete profiles, race reports, and shoe and gear reviews. He coached adult runners with the New York Road Runners in the 1990s and has coached junior high and high school cross-country and track during the past 12 years. He has run 26 marathons with a best time of 2:46:04. His books and articles reflect his love of running, his depth of knowledge of the sport, his breadth of interests, and his continual quest to answer Why? and So what?